The Relief of Mafeking

Filson Young

Complete & Unabridged

Tutis Digital Publishing Private Limited

First published in 1900 as *The Relief of Mafeking*.

CONTENTS

Preface

The proprietors of the *Manchester Guardian* have kindly allowed me to make use of their copyright in the letters written by me to that newspaper during the first half of the year. The substance of the letters has been reproduced in the hope that home-staying folk may find in them something of the atmosphere that surrounds the collision of armed forces. It is a strange and rude atmosphere; yet it pleases me at this moment to remember not so much the strangeness and rudeness as the kindness and good-fellowship that made a dreadful business tolerable and the memory of it pleasant. Many friends of these brave days I may not see again, but if their eyes should ever light on this page I would have them know that it contains a greeting.

FILSON YOUNG

LONDON, *July 31st, 1900*

PART I

England in Time of War

CHAPTER I

How the Reserves Came Up

From a seat in the paymaster's office of the depôt barracks at Bury one afternoon in November, 1899, I could look either into the barrack yard or out along the Bolton Road. A four-wheeler clove its way through the crowd surrounding the gates, and the sentries presented arms to it. It contained my friend, the paymaster, who presently came upstairs carrying a bag in which were several hundred pounds sterling – the real sinews of war. This was the man whose business it was to call up the Reservists, and he had a very simple way of doing it. He had several books containing large forms divided by perforation into four parts. The first was a counterfoil on which was written the Reservist's name and the date of posting the order; the second was a railway warrant requesting the railway company to furnish him with a ticket available by the most direct route from his place of residence to the depôt; the third was the order requiring him to present himself at the barracks on or before a certain date; and the fourth was a money-order for three shillings, officially called an advance, but virtually a present from a considerate Government. On the 11th of the month the paymaster at Bury had signed about six hundred of these notices, and had seen them posted; on Sunday and Monday they had begun to fall like bombs on the breakfast tables of prosperous civilians all over the country; and soon the pieces of blue paper had made a sad disturbance in several hundreds of cottage homes, and added several hundred men to the strength of the 2nd Battalion of the Lancashire Fusiliers. The business of the pay office, or at least my friend's part of it – a few subalterns rushing up in a hurry to get money for their various companies; eighty pounds for A, a hundred pounds for D, and so on – was soon over, and then he told me something of how the Reserve system works.

All the men in the Reserve have put in at least seven years' service. They go into the Reserve first for a term of five years at sixpence a day, and then (if they wish) for a term of four years at fourpence a day. Of course when the Reserves are called out they receive the same pay as regular soldiers, and their wives have separation allowances. As everyone knows, this was the first time that any considerable number of the

Reserves had been called up, and the system has worked admirably. About 98 per cent, in some districts presented themselves, the small remainder being either ill or in gaol. A small proportion of those who came up were rejected by the doctor, but on the whole the men were tough and fit. In this district they were allowed eight days in which to settle their affairs and present themselves at the depôt, but most of them did not come until the last minute, and several not until after the last minute of the time allowed by the order.

The crowd outside the barrack gates was composed chiefly of women and loafers, but every now and then it opened to admit a handful of reluctant-looking men, who had probably stayed outside until their money was exhausted. And many of them were hanging about outside the gates having nothing to do and no money to spend, but deferring to the last moment the final step of self-submission to the iron hand of discipline. For once the Reservist was inside the barrack yard he could have no more liberty, probably, for many a long month – unless, indeed, he gained an endless liberty on the battlefield. The scene through the opposite window looking on to the barrack yard was very different from the rather sombre picture without. The yard was gay with the wonderful red that has done so much to make the army popular. For movement there were a few squads of Militia recruits being drilled by the trumpet-voiced sergeants; and for music there was the ring of a hundred rifle-butts striking the ground together, the tramp and click of many feet, and the clatter of the colonel's horse as he rode across the yard.

But the most interesting people were the Reservists and their friends, who dotted the yard in many-coloured groups. Here was a party of girls and women taking a farewell of some engaging blade whose course of gallantry had been suddenly interrupted. There was a father standing with his wife and small family grouped round him, no one saying very much, but everyone feeling a good deal. And another group would be laughing and singing, not quite recovered from the means they had taken to drown regrets.

Sitting in the window, one could trace the Reservist's progress from his entrance at the gate to his disappearance into quarters. The square was filled with little processions containing six or eight men each; first from the orderly-room to the hospital, in all kinds of civilian raiment: black, grey, brown, green, blue, drab – anything but red; hatless, capless, black-hatted, cloth-capped, shabby, spruce, dirty, soiled, clean, pretty clean, white-faced, red-faced, unkempt, well-groomed, hungry, well-fed, thin, fat – every class between clerks and tramps; every condition between prosperity and destitution. A procession was also constantly flowing from the hospital to the quartermaster's stores – the same procession, with one military touch; for this time the men did not straggle, but were marched single file in charge of a sergeant. The next procession was from the stores to the men's quarters; but now each man had a great bundle under his arms containing his entire kit wrapped up in an overcoat.

The quartermaster, not without pardonable pride, took me over the stores in which the men's kits are prepared. There were hundreds of racks containing bundles so cunningly rolled that you could see at a glance what was in each. And beside each bundle was a valise already packed with everything that a campaigner could need; indeed, when I read the printed list showing what was in each my heart warmed with the same joy that I felt when I first read *Robinson Crusoe*. Government, who is rigorous and unyielding as a disciplinarian to her soldiers, is a mother to them in her provision for their wants. Each bag contained a knife, fork, spoon, tin canteen, shaving brush, soap, razor, boot brushes, clothes brush, hair brush, pipeclay, button polisher, cleaning paste, and a dozen other things just as interesting and as useful. Out of curiosity I opened a housewife, and my heart was touched with the almost feminine consideration that it indicated; for there, cunningly folded up, were skeins of wool and cotton in many different shades, as well as half a dozen sizes of needles. Surely the War Office is human, and not the strange machine that some of us esteem it, for how else could it provide that Tommy shall not have to darn his socks with scarlet, nor his tunic with grey, nor his trousers with white wool? As the men came into the stores each one received his share of these excellent things, and the quartermaster's sergeants displayed quite a genius in estimating and fitting the various proportions of the men. And the men's eyes brightened at the sight of the glorious new red cloth; I believe that, although they wore it for a few days only, it did much to reconcile them with the inconvenience and hardship that some of them endured in rejoining. Khaki uniforms were served out later.

All round the barrack square the men stood in groups as I have described, and in one corner were clusters of men arrayed in their new garments. One could read pretty easily in their faces the story of the last few days. One saw several men who had evidently risen in the world since they had left the army. They had an air of sleekness and delicacy that made them seem out of place. Others had evidently been going down in the social scale, and wore their new clothes like fine feathers. Some were evidently glad at the prospect of action and excitement, and fell back into the regimental routine as a man sits down in a comfortable chair. To others, not a few, all this hustle was an act in a domestic tragedy. Sometimes it was a comedy, as in the case of one man who had built up a "nice little butchering business," snatching his profits from the niggard hand of competition; and now he must go forth to kill men, leaving his rival master in the field of domestic butchery. But the comedies were few, or else I did not come across them, for it was the serious side of this business that impressed me the most. Men caught away from new-found family joys, not for personal advancement or glory, but to take their places as units in the huge war-machine that is fed with human bodies. It is so easy to speak and think of "losses" when we count them by the hundred; it is so hard and bitter to think of one death and all that it means when one stands and speaks to a soldier. I found one man standing apart by himself – a young man, with a good, clean, hardy face – and there were tears in his eyes. As I was passing he asked me what time it was, and in a few minutes he told me his story. He had been married two years; he had one little child; he had left his wife dying of pneumonia. That was all; but I think one can hardly realise how much it meant. I should like some civilians who do their soldiering in an armchair, and who really seem to like a war for the spice with which it flavours their newspaper, to have seen that man and heard his short tale of misery.[1]He is, of course, one of the few on whom an admirable system inflicts a fearful wound; but he is an example (if one were needed) of the matchless discipline that can teach a man to obey without question or complaint a command that has two edges for death. I am glad to say that I met no other man in half so dreadful a plight as his, but there were dozens of men to whom the order came as an ending of happiness, and of course one knew, although the thought was not dwelt upon, that many of the little homes of which these men had been the centre and support would have that support no more. Yet of one thing I am very sure. Not one of the men to whom I spoke but was willing and anxious to serve his country; not one but looked proud to be wearing the old uniform again. The sadness and trouble was all in the retrospect, not in the outlook. Tommy Atkins, with his great, simple, conspicuous vices and his obscure, surprising, and enduring virtues was unconsciously putting into practice the precept of a certain Old Buccaneer: *No regrets; they unman the heart we want for to-morrow.*

---

[1] This man's wife died a week after he had sailed.

CHAPTER II

How the Army Left England

The few days that elapsed between rejoining and embarkation were spent by the Reservist at the depôt barracks of his regiment, where he received his kit and underwent the small amount of drill necessary to remove the rust of civilian life. After that, the sound of reveille in the depth of a winter night; the sudden awakening; the hasty breakfast, eaten like a Passover feast; the long and noisy railway journey; the faint, salt smell of the sea, and the first sight of it through the rainy dawn. In the early days of the war I was present at many embarkations at Liverpool and Southampton, and they left an impression on my mind which will not easily be effaced. For, even to an onlooker, the embarkation of troops, with its sights and sounds of tragedy, is an affair that burns itself into the memory; one is dazzled and confounded by the number and variety of the small dramas that are enacted before one's eyes; and the whole is framed in a setting of military system and circumstance that lends dignity, if that were needed, to the humble tragedies of the moment.

Only a few of the thousands who came to watch the departure of the *Canada* from Liverpool one December morning were allowed inside the dock shed; nearly all of those within the gate were sweethearts and wives and children of soldiers who had contrived to procure passes for them. Even in the shed the scene was one of extraordinary confusion. At intervals of about half an hour detachments were marched in and formed up at one end of the shed, where they left their bundles and heavy kit, and whence they were marched in single file up the gangway of the ship. With the exception of the Manchesters, all the troops were in khaki, and were easily distinguishable from the dark-coloured mass of civilians. Thus there was always a yellow pool of colour in the midst of the black mass, and all the morning a thin yellow line flowed from the pool to the ship's gangway. As often as one looked, during the whole morning, there was a line of men in the act of ascending the gangway. One felt as though one had fallen asleep for a moment and dreamed, and waked again to find the same men in the same position, so little did the appearance of things change. It was really a picture that one looked at, for the colours and bold outlines remained constant; the eye at times grew used to the minute movement, and refused to notice that the picture was preserved only because the same things were being done over and over again by hundreds of different people. The same

5

greetings as friends recognised the newly-arrived man, the same hurried words, the same faltering voices, the same desperate embraces, the same endless tramp from the formed ranks to the ship, the same tears. The absorption of so many acute personal emotions into one revolving routine was the most amazing part of it; the stream of discipline and system ran swift and deep here, drawing into its flood even the most sacred and intimate of human experiences, and turning into a pattern the parting of husband from wife and father from child. When at length one became used to the picture one began to notice the elements of its composition, and only in watching them could one gain relief from the overburdening sense of personality submerged in a system. The little dramas were very strange and very affecting. I can only give a few examples out of dozens that I watched.

As the troops came in at the door, marching four deep, the crowd formed on each side, and those who had friends in the detachment tried to get a prominent place in the front rank of the crowd, where they could attract the attention of the soldiers as they passed. The men were not hurried, and they were marching at ease, so there was generally time for a few words and a kiss or a hand-clasp before they were moved on. One wife, who was little more than a girl, had taken a good place on the edge of the crowd when her husband's detachment began to file in. I heard her telling a friend that she had not said good-bye to "her lad," as she wanted to see the last of him; it had been arranged that she was to be near when he passed so that he could give her a parting kiss. Oh, how anxiously she scanned the faces of the men as they swung into sight, throwing all her soul into her eyes!

Presently, "There he is!" she cried; "here, Jim, I'm here!"

The young man's fine honest face had a look no less intent than hers, but it was turned away from her; he was searching as eagerly as she, but on the wrong side of the lane of people; and by one of those impish tricks that Fate plays upon us in acute moments, he never saw her, nor heard her voice above the cheers of the people and the blare of the band. It was a cruel thing; she was fast wedged in the crowd. Someone ran after the man and told him where she was, but before the sympathiser could reach him his company had been drawn up and he could not be allowed to fall out. And long before she was clear of the tightly packed throng he had passed on to the ship, where she could not follow him.

Another incident of another kind. The North Lancashires were marching in, and an old man in the crowd was on the look-out for his son. He explained to everybody near him what a fine boy his son was, and how keen a soldier; how it had nearly broken the old man's heart that his boy should leave him and go to the war, but how it would "do un good and make a mon of un." Presently two soldiers appeared, half-carrying and half-dragging between them a young man who was so drunk that he could neither stand nor walk. His helmet was jammed over his eyes, but as he was dragged past us it fell off and rolled to the old man's feet. I heard him draw in his breath sharply and murmur something as his face flushed; and then all the people round began to point and say, "That's his son there, him that's being carried"; and some – God forgive them! – laughed and joked at the old man. And he who had a moment ago filled our ears with the praises of his boy gazed after him with a look of bitter amazement and then went silently away. Another man who had missed seeing his wife before he had embarked caught sight of her from the ship's deck as she stood upon the quay with tears in her eyes. There was no chance of his being allowed to pass down the gangway. But the husband in him knew no obedience to the stern order, and he dived clean off the stern of the steamer into the filthy water and swam, khaki and all, to the steps at the side of the dock. And you may be sure his wife was there to help him out, and she forgot her grief in her pride at his daring. So he held her in his arm for a moment (and had three ringing cheers from his mates into the bargain) before he was collared and marched back to restraint, dirty but glorious.

Here and there one saw men much the worse for liquor; and I have no words to describe the folly of those friends who thrust bottles of spirits into the soldiers' hands as they passed through the streets. They did them a double cruelty, for the poor fellows, all unstrung by their partings, gulped the raw spirit thinking they drank courage; and so once or twice I saw poor women saying good-bye to staggering maniacs – grim mockeries of the husbands they might never see again, the poor fools themselves at present oblivious indeed, but doomed to I know not what horrors of remorse on awaking. Happily, however, there were not many in this sad condition. Most of the men behaved with a fortitude and gentleness that was most touching. Indeed I find it hard to express my admiration of their bearing. There was none of the bluster of the armchair Jingo, none of the loud hectoring and swaggering and bravado that distinguish the carpet warrior. On the contrary, when they were talking of the war amongst themselves they had an air of quiet determination, of good-humoured banter, and of easy, serious confidence far more ominous for an enemy than any amount of fluent rant. After the world of politics, with its hair-splitting and word-mincing, it was good to be with soldiers – the men who do the work.

They knew no fine political shades, they bandied no epithets; England was at war and they were going to fight – that was enough. And the spirit in which they fought all the world knows: every day during the war one read tales of devotion and heroism that became almost commonplace; it is even a commonplace to praise them. Yet one could not see the soldiers in this most trying duty of all, the laying down of home ties and interests (for I think the heroism of mere fighting is nothing to it), without feeling a pride in the moral discipline that makes it all possible, and under the authority of which Tommy is content to be as a child. And this childlike submission to discipline has its pathetic side, as when one saw the little family of mother and children grouped to see the last of its head. The children stood in wide-eyed amazement to see daddy the Reservist, who in the little household had been the emblem of all authority, now in the place of obedience, and taking directions from another man (not so big and strong as he) as to how he should stand and into what hole he should put the buckle of his strap. Thus even the father and the husband are absorbed in the soldier. It is a great price; and the way in which it was paid by so many was perhaps our firmest assurance of the stuff that is in our soldiers.

Early on the morning of departure a few hundred people – mostly women – stood on the pierhead of Canada Dock, watching the transport as she lay a short distance off in the stream with the Blue Peter at her fore and the St. George's ensign hanging astern. The rain beat steadily down, loading the raw wind that blew out of the morning twilight, and the brown water broke sullenly to the send of a setting flood tide. The faces of nearly all the women were worn with weeping; now they wept no longer, but looked dully out to sea, while the rain ran down their soaking garments and splashed on the ground. A drunken soldier who had somehow got ashore the night before reeled helplessly on his wife's arm, his head bruised and cut and his new uniform torn and filthy. But in the woman's face there was a kind of fearful joy; she had rescued him from his pot-house satellites, and she thought she could keep him. Presently a tug came off from the transport with a picket to collect deserters – he had to go. She sobbed and wailed, imploring the sergeant in vain; and she clung to her poor senseless husband as though she would never leave him. He hardly knew her; he laughed vacantly in her face when with streaming eyes she begged him to speak her name; then they took him away from her. As the tug steamed out I heard him singing.

A little while afterwards the *Canada's* siren began to wail and squeal with a horrible mockery of painful cries. The tugs backed clear of her, and lent their shrill voices to the discordant concert. Presently the water astern of the transport turned from brown to foaming white, and her masts began to move past the farther shore. There was a faint sound of cheering from her, but she was soon out of sound and sight, and still the women stared into the mist that had enfolded her, as though their wishes might draw her back again. But in a little while they turned towards home and a world that had changed its face.

On another day I went down to Liverpool to see the *Majestic* depart with troops for the front. The weather was consistently unkind. The *Canada* had sailed in a whirl of rainy fog, and the departing passengers of the *Majestic* looked across a little inky strip of water to a land that was cloaked with snow. It was bitterly cold on the landing-stage, and all the interest of the scene could not keep the bitter wind from whipping one's face and numbing the feet. The wooden planks resounded not more with the tramp of marching feet than with the hard stampings of people who were trying to restore circulation. There were no very poor people on the stage. The space opposite to the ship was occupied chiefly by the friends of officers and by the troops themselves, and certainly it seemed kinder to the men to prevent the dreadful scrambling for farewells that took place when the *Canada* sailed. But a sea of anxious faces pressed against the barriers at either end of the reserved space, and no doubt there was much bitter envy of us in the enclosure, who had so much better an opportunity, and perhaps so much less reasonable a claim to the front places.

Outwardly this departure seemed very different from that of the *Canada*. It was not so sordid, if one may use the term; the vessel did not slip away furtively from a dock in the small hours of the morning, but departed in open day from the more accessible landing-stage; and although the weather was chill and bitter, it had not that infinitely dreary effect upon the spirits that one associates with a soaking downpour. Here were all the pomps and circumstances of farewell – the blowing of bands and wavings of caps and great shouts of a multitude that must give vent to acute emotions. Yet, different though the outward circumstances were, they only accentuated the likeness that lay beneath. Good-bye is good-bye, whether we say it at a carriage window or shout it across a strip of harbour water; whether a crowd sings "Auld Lang Syne" or a mother whispers "Don't forget me." And at the sailing of the *Majestic*, with all its dignity, one saw the same tragedies repeated over and over again, until one's heart sickened of it all, and one would gladly have come away. Of course it was not among the officers and their wives that one saw these things; people used to self-control keep their griefs to themselves, and perhaps a very inexperienced person would have been deceived by the smiles on women's faces and the cheery chaff of men. Even here there were things to be seen at the last moment, but I confess that I turned my back when the saloon gangway was about to be removed; some things are sacred even from the man whose business it is to describe what he sees.

It was after the two thousand troops had all been embarked that the friends of the men were admitted to the stage, and the dismal, though enthusiastic, part of the affair began. Before that everything was business and order. As the men arrived they were provided with hot coffee and meat pies, which they drank and ate with every sign of pleasure. Some of us who were very cold envied them for that moment. The forward gangway was for about an hour occupied by men who did nothing but pass rifles from the quay to the ship; it was a formidable sight, this stream of deadly weapons that flowed on board. Up another gangway enough cordite to blow up the whole of Liverpool was being gingerly carried in small cases. But this hour or two of embarkation, in which so much really happened, left little impression on my mind. It simply was one more illustration of the admirable efficiency of discipline for which our army is famous. It was when the gangways were removed and the crowd began to pour on to the stage that the affair became human; and the half-hour that elapsed between that time and the moment when the mist finally hid the ship wrote itself much more deeply on my memory.

One gangway was left open, and stragglers and men who at the last moment had stayed away for an hour with their wives and children were hunted out and hurried up it. At the shore end there were many painful scenes, which people with a little imagination may picture for themselves. Fortunately a farewell is a brief thing, and leaves only aching hearts; people could not stand a sustained agony like that of the last moment. It is the price we pay for our powers of memory and forethought; the charger, going perhaps to a bloody and cruel death, steps willingly enough up plank; the drunken man sings his good-bye; only the sober and alert taste the fearful sting of parting. Even the people who had kept up a great show of callousness had the mask suddenly and for the moment plucked from their faces; young subalterns with rather watery eyes and very loud voices ran swiftly up the plank, and brave women who had a smile even to the last for their husbands turned a different face shorewards. One could not help contrasting the weight of the burden for those who went away and those who stayed behind; for the men and for the women; for those who were going to fight, to die perhaps, but still to *do* something, and for those who had nothing but their thoughts to be busy with. Pessimistic as this view may seem, it is the true one; the event described as an "enthusiastic send-off" is essentially a melancholy function, and the relief afforded by the antics of a few intoxicated men does not make it less so. It is strange, indeed, how important a part is played by the whisky-bottle in the farewells of the poor. I have seen it passed round family circles at the last moment like some grotesque sacrament; have even overheard husband and wife almost quarrelling in their desire to press the comforter each upon the other. "Here, take it with you, Sam." "No, Missus, you 'ave it; I can get some off Tom." "No, lad, take it – I'll throw it after you if you don't." Chance generally stepped in to kill the ghost in the bottle, throwing it to the ground and spilling the contents. I saw one little boy, aged about four, run up to his daddy at the last moment with a gorgeous present in the shape of a glass pistol (a delicate reference to his profession) full of spirits; it had a cork in the barrel, and I suppose you fired it down your throat. Amid all these scenes the officers displayed an unvarying tact, coaxing the men on board and not unduly hastening their farewells; but for all that there were many violent and tragic scenes.

Just before the last gangway was run ashore a little woman came up, crying and almost breathless, and begging to be allowed to say good-bye to her husband, who was at the other end of the gangway, not allowed to come down. The orders were absolute – no one must go up to the ship. Then the woman broke out into a great wailing and sobbing, praying the quartermaster on her knees that he would let her go half-way up the gangway; but he was as firm as a rock. Then she came to the edge of the landing-stage and cried quietly, all alone in that vast crowd, now and then calling broken words of endearment to the man who stood a dozen yards away from her across the strip of black water. Discipline is heavy, and crushes; it is also sharp, and sometimes cuts cruelly and deeply. But in the midst of her amazing grief she found time to call some cheering words across to her husband: "Keep your heart up, lad, and think of me and the children as loves you." He, poor soul, looked thunder at his sergeant, and raged and swore; but he was a unit in a mass – he kicked against the pricks, and he knew it.

At last the gangway was removed, and a kind of quietness fell upon the crowd, waiting for the next harrowing sensation. It came in a succession of those minute incidents that burn themselves into the memory of people whose nerves are on the rack. The splash of a hawser into the dock; the deep notes of the engine-room telegraph, and the clicking reply upon the bridge; the spinning of the wheel as a quartermaster tests the steering engine; the clack and spit of winches, and finally the thrilling shout of the foghorn, whose echo leaves you trembling – all these things have a painful significance, and they bite and grip into the heart. As the ship began to move a band on the shade-deck struck up "Auld Lang Syne," and immediately the floodgates were unlocked. Tears started again into bitterly dry eyes, handkerchiefs were waved, people shouted, sang snatches of song – everyone made a sound of some kind, and contributed to the great unrestrained noise of human beings in distress and excitement. Above it all rose the hooting of foghorns and sirens, while the band made its noise too – thump and throb of drums, scream of pipes, and red-hot flare of brass instruments. Sea-birds, seeing the ship about to depart, flapped and hovered about it by the score, adding their shrill cries to the tumult; and high on his flying-bridge stood the captain, shifting his telegraph from "stand by" to "ahead," holding up or moving his hand, but not uttering his voice. It was a striking picture, in which he stood as an image of a Fate by which all men were for the moment helplessly crushed down.

It was at this moment that something happened which I, for one, had been expecting. One of the many men who were perched in the rigging or outside the rails lost his hold, and in the same second was wriggling in the water. It conveys some idea of the pitch to which the crowd was strung up to say that the noise did not increase and hardly changed its character. I suppose people turned from cheering to shouting, but the big sound was still the same, and since the bands-men were high up and in the middle of the deck they saw and knew nothing and went on playing. But something else impressed me far more deeply; indeed, I think that I can never forget it. Quite close to me was standing the man's wife holding a baby, and as the man's face turned towards us in his floundering she said calmly, "God, it's my George." And the little boy, not understanding, repeated gleefully and senselessly, "It's dadda; it's dadda."

I looked at the woman's face; her cup had been full before; she had drunk her fill of grief; and this new horror, her husband struggling like a mouse in the bitter cold water, could not add a pang to her torture. All that I have described happened, of course, in a few seconds; the man had barely gone under before one of the ship's butchers, in his white clothes, was in after him. Let no one belittle the race of butchers. The life-taker knew how to save life, and Master Butcher had his man in a moment, turned him on his back, and began to swim ashore; indeed, there was no fear of the man's drowning, for there were half a dozen men in the water within half a minute of the accident. The man was brought ashore, and his wife helped to rub him down; only to go through her parting again on the deck of a tender a few minutes afterwards. But there was a cheerier note in the cheering that broke out when the ship again began to move, and when the band struck up "God

Save the Queen" everyone who had a croak in him or her joined with a will. The shape of the ship grew dim in the mist, but still the sea-birds cried and hovered like winged prayers and wishes between her and the shore.

In the Thames and at Southampton similar scenes were enacted almost daily. Here is an account of a "Specimen Day" at Southampton – one of the busiest that had been known there since the beginning of the war, for Lord Roberts's grand army was being hurried out to repair the fortunes shattered at Magersfontein, Stormberg, and Colenso.

All day long crowded troop-trains had been steaming into the station, where small pilot engines waited to receive them and drag them, groaning and squealing, round the curves and across the points that lead to the docks. The first train arrived at about nine, and the last at two. Between those hours there was a constant succession of trains. Three steamers were waiting to receive the troops; the Peninsular and Oriental liner *Assaye*, the Union Steamship Company's *Goorkha*, and the Castle liner *Braemar Castle*. The *Assaye* was a new boat, and this was her maiden voyage. She carried two regiments, the 2nd Norfolk and the 2nd Hampshire, and the fact that the Hampshire is the territorial regiment of the port, accounted for the unusually large crowd that assembled on the wharf beside which the *Assaye* lay. The business of despatching transports had become so commonplace at Southampton that unless there was some special interest attached to the embarkation there was no crowd at all. Only the town loafers would assemble in any strength. But many of the Southampton people had friends in the Hampshire Regiment, so there were some thousands pressing round the barriers that surrounded the dock shed into which the trains on arriving were drawn.

It was on board the *Assaye* that I spent the greater part of the morning and afternoon, piloted by a naval lieutenant who was in charge of the embarkation. I perched myself high up on the flying-bridge and watched the busy scene below. In the next dock was the *Goorkha*, into whose commodious maw were pouring the 2nd Lincolnshire Regiment, the 9th Field Company Royal Engineers, the 14th Brigade Staff, the Cavalry Brigade Field Hospital, the Fifth Division Field Hospital, and No. 12 Company Army Medical Corps. Further away, alongside the dock extension jetty, the *Braemar Castle* was receiving the 1st King's Own Scottish Borderers, No. 7 Bearer Company, and No. 19 Company Army Medical Corps. In the *Assaye*, however, were men of only two colours, the Norfolks and the Hampshires. The Norfolks arrived first, and were promptly embarked. The 'tween-decks of the *Assaye*, having been constructed specially for the purpose, were more commodious than those on most other transports, and certainly they were better ventilated, for a great open shaft ran right up from the bottom of the ship to the upper deck, and round this were grouped the tables at which the men, in messes of sixteen, were to be accommodated. The men seemed pleased with their quarters and with the general arrangements made for their comfort, but they were almost laughably critical. The fact was that the soldiers were in great danger of being spoiled by the fuss that had been made of them before they embarked. It is well that we should cheer the soldiers up by our enthusiasm, but, as everyone knows, the British public did much more than that. "Tommy Atkins" was the rage for the moment, and what may be called "Absent-minded Beggarism" was rampant. Unfortunately, this enthusiasm found a vent too often in silly and thoughtless squandering of money on the soldiers. They were banqueted before they started; their friends used to ply them with drink; mayors were waiting upon them at every turn with pipes and tobacco, and total strangers showered money on them quite recklessly. For example, while I was on the *Assaye's* bridge I saw a civilian, standing quite apart from the crowd, with his hat full of copper and small silver coins. No one seemed to be watching him. He could have no thought of making an impression. But in an ecstasy of enthusiasm he kept throwing showers of money to the troops on deck. It is an excellent thing that the people at home should be touched with such gratitude to the men who fight for them, but, like all great public movements which have more heart than head in them, this kind of thing was sometimes overdone, and failed in its object. One saw the men sometimes arriving drunken, grumbling, and impudent; criticising the quality or quantity of the refreshments which the steamship company had thoughtfully provided for them, and generally behaving in a way most unlike what one would expect. No one seemed to lack money, although so much was spent in drink. Several times that day I heard men at the canteen calling for whisky and soda or brandy and potash, and grumbling heartily when they were not supplied.

With regard to the way in which men got drink one or two things fall to be said. Every effort was made by the authorities to prevent drunkenness. One of the naval embarkation officers told me that drink was not supplied to the men at the canteen, that they were forbidden to bring any on board, and that they were forbidden to buy or receive any from civilians; yet it had been found that certain tradesmen at Southampton had deliberately smuggled whisky on board by heavily bribing some of the crew. In the face of this kind of thing the officers could do little. They spoke very bitterly of the cruelty to the men involved in such practices, for the soldiers are necessarily packed pretty close together when hammocks are slung, and when the effects of drunkenness are added to the horrors of sea-sickness the result is awful, and almost unendurable by a man who cherishes any self-respect. I mention this at some length because, although it was not prominent on the day of which I am writing, it had happened terribly often, and on the day before it had made the scene at the embarkation of an Irish regiment a really horrible one. The two regiments which embarked on the *Assaye* happened to be the soberest I had yet seen. Indeed, there was hardly one case of drunkenness amongst them. I think this was partly because the outside public was not allowed near the ship. The men passed from the train directly on board, and did not come in contact with their friends. It was kinder to the friends too. I saw none of those heartrending tragic scenes of parting, none of the wild grief that grows so much wilder for being indulged. From the officers' deck the picture of embarkation appeared in outline rather than in detail. The constant movement of people far below, the orderly disorder, the shouts and cries of officers and stevedores, the waving arms of cranes and the general excitement produced in a mere onlooker a strange sense of isolation. One felt like Gulliver observing the Liliputians in some great effort of maritime preparation, and the longer one looked the smaller and more like toy soldiers seemed the men. Such an endless stream of them poured from the dock shed to the ship. I heard their cries faintly. "Bring back old Kroojer's whiskers" was the burden of them, and this was indeed the chief trophy, the chief spoil of war which the average soldier pictured for himself. It was strange to think that this army of Liliput which tramped and cried down there conceived its mission so vaguely and imperfectly that it could depart light-heartedly.

The deep note of the *Goorkha's* foghorn sounded close at hand. The tops of her masts glided past the roof of the dock shed; in five minutes she was out of sight, and her departure seemed to have been almost uncelebrated. She got away at about two, and an hour later the *Braemar Castle* also departed.

The only thing which now delayed the departure of the *Assaye* was the embarkation of the horses. There were eight chargers belonging to officers of the two regiments, and they made the utmost objection to being enclosed in narrow boxes and swung in mid-air. In particular a magnificent grey belonging to the colonel of the Hampshire Regiment gave any amount of trouble. It took her groom ten minutes to coax her into the box, and as soon as it began to move upwards she snorted and trembled with fear, and finally sat down on her haunches, with her neck hanging over the door. The colonel, who was standing near, seemed rather proud of this exhibition, but when the mare was almost beside herself with terror, and while she was yet swinging in mid-air, he spoke reassuring words – "Woa, Bunny! Steady, old girl!" The beast could not see him, but she heard the voice in the air, and became suddenly quiet. May she live to need the same assurance on her homeward journey, was one's involuntary thought. The sight of these fine horses was very pitiful, in the light of their possible destiny. One looked at the glossy coats and saw them torn and bloody. One watched the nervous wild eye and the twitching ears, and heard the whistling bullets and the shells bursting round them, who know no reason for the commotion, holding themselves bravely in check until the steadying voice behind them ceases and the load suddenly lightens, or until a stray bullet ends both fears and endeavours.

After many delays the last horse was on board. And now there remained only the inspection by the naval embarkation officers, an interval for the crowd of half an hour, which the band on the quay did its best to pass agreeably. There were many false alarms of departure. Every patriotic song and tune had been played and cheered, but after "Auld Lang Syne" had been hammered out for the third time the ship began to move. As she left the quay the younger men at one end of the ship made a great commotion. One held up a flag which he proposed to plant on "Kroojer's Hill." (Some authorities might read Majuba.) These men, recruits for the most part, made in their ignorance of war a joyful noise, but the Reservists and old hands looked grave and sad, and hardly joined in the singing or cheering. They were thinking.

CHAPTER III

How the Wounded Came Home

Going down Southampton Water on January 5th to meet the *Aurania* with her company of sick and wounded, one enjoyed a wonderful study of sober tints in land and sea under a winter sky. The little steamer clove light green waters that were hardly rippled by the breeze. This green sea she divided in two long curling lines that seemed to reach the shore on either hand, merging their light colour with a dark green of fields waiting for spring. The fields in their turn faded into the bluish black of leafless trees, and the trees bounded a sky of soft banks shading from blue to grey. The waters seemed almost deserted, except for a ship that now and then might meet us, stealing up on the tide and gently heeling to the breeze. Sometimes a yacht would pass us, sometimes a fishing-smack; but it was a lonely journey. The air was soft and sweet − not like that of spring, but like that of a world which lives in the promise of a coming spring and can wait. There were no sounds but one sweet and familiar − the whisper, swelling and diminishing but never dying, of foam at the cutwater.

Little Hythe seemed to have retired into itself for the winter. Its pier was deserted by boats and men when we passed. Lower down on the other side was Netley Hospital, with how many pains and agonies hidden behind its long, imposing front. Opposite Netley the sea eats and bites like an acid into a kind of mossy grass of rare and vivid green, making a wonderful coast-line on a small scale, with bays and channels and sounds.

We made for West Cowes, where the sea brims up to the streets and the spray sometimes sprinkles the shop windows. Here the telegraph was set in motion, asking Hurst Castle for news of the *Aurania*. But there was no news, so, as it would take her two hours to reach Southampton after passing the Castle, we went on past green promontories that dip into the sea, right up to where the trees clothe them, past the towers of Osborne, to Ryde. Again the telegraph asked the question, and again there was a negative answer. Then we cut across the Solent towards Southsea, watching the weird evolutions of a 35-knot torpedo-boat. It darted about, annihilating the small distances of the Solent and making a strange, buzzing noise like some foul fly. Vomiting flames and sparks, it trailed a cloud in the air and snow upon the water. While we were crawling across the river it had made a dozen journeys. Now it would be down near Cowes, and now half-way up Southampton Water, and when one looked again a few minutes afterwards it would be close astern, overtaking us with the speed of a nightmare. I escaped from it at Southsea, for there the wires told me something that sent me doubling to the railway station, and thanking my stars that I was in time for a fast train to Southampton. It arrived at half-past three, and at four the *Aurania* showed her nose round the corner of a dock shed. Ten minutes later she was alongside and berthed, and the disembarkation began.

The total absence of any kind of popular demonstration was most impressive. There was no crowd at all, and the barriers that had been provided were not needed. This neglect of a welcome seemed sadly to discount the value of the great hysterical demonstrations made when the troops departed. They were men who were perhaps going to suffer for their country. These invalids had suffered for it, and no one came to cheer them up. Of course some of the men's own friends were there, and the few strangers who were present shook hands with the men as they came limping and hopping and stumbling down the gangway. But it was all very quiet, very sad, very tame from a spectator's point of view, but deeply significant. One could hardly imagine a greater contrast than was presented by the same shed on a day of departure and on a day of arrival like this. In the one case great crowds hurrahing and shouting and cheering, bands playing, and bottles going busily round. In the other a great quietness, a few people standing in little knots and speaking almost in undertones. And the men themselves were very different. No excitement, of course; no drunkenness; no yelling for "Kroojer's whiskers." Oh, no! – something very different from that. About a hundred men with pain-worn faces, bandaged arms and legs, slings and splints everywhere, and talking, when they talked at all, of the horrors of the war, of the death of comrades, and of the seriousness of the news we gave them, in the light of their own experiences at the front. The men were speedily disembarked and taken into the dock shed where a train with some ambulance coaches was waiting, but they preferred to stand and talk for a little while before taking their seats. A really kind and useful work was done by members of the Southampton branch of the "Absent-minded Beggars" relief corps, who provided hot coffee and buns for the men, and in addition provided each with a stamped telegraph form, so that he might reassure his friends at home.

Of course there was another beside the serious aspect of this scene. Nothing could exceed the interest in their ailments displayed by the men who had partly recovered from them, and those whose wounds had healed could not tire of giving demonstrations to their friends and relations, or even to strangers. An illness or a wound is often the first view an ignorant man gets of Nature's ingenuity displayed in the construction of his own person, and when one of these invalids got hold of some medical or surgical word he would cherish and roll it on his tongue like a man tasting wine. One of them – a man who looked as strong as a horse – was explaining to an admiring group how he came to be alive at all. A bullet had passed through the rim of his helmet, entered his left temple, passed behind his nose, through the roof of his mouth, and out through the lower part of his right cheek. First he would show us the dent in his temple; then describe, with many strange words, the inward passage of the bullet; and then, emerging into the sphere of common things, wind up with, "and came out of my blooming cheek." Then he would show the dent in his cheek, and pass his helmet round for all to see, as a conjurer does. I moved round with this man and heard him recite his tale three times, and every time he used just the same form of words, which he repeated pat like a lesson. His corruption of "cerebral" was amusing. "Nearly scattered the cerveral nerve, so help me!" he said. One could have understood it if he had been in the Spanish-American war. Another soldier used a word which I cannot explain. He was showing a mate how a bullet had entered his shoulder, "and," said he, "it penetrated me agamemnon." What is an agamemnon? It has been puzzling me ever since.

Only a few of the more robust men were going on in this way, and there was enough of the pathetic even in the man with the "cerveral" nerve and him with the "agamemnon." The men looked tired and serious, and seemed to lack interest in anything but their own afflictions. It is almost a pity that the public will not witness such scenes as this, for I fear that it is still sadly in need of having even the most elementary fruits of war brought home to it. One might, of course, easily overdraw the picture of the men's condition; it is difficult to describe it faithfully. Many of them seemed happy and contented to be home again, and forgot past pains in present joy. As I turned away from the carriage window I heard a confused drone of conversation, in which such terms as "ligature," "suppuration," "cavity of the hear'ole," "styptic," and "prelatic" were prominent. The last thing I heard was – "He hadn't got no fraxur at all, leastways only a simple un. Mine was a compound fraxur." One can understand these things. But what is an "agamemnon"?

It was dark when the train went away, and there was nothing more for me to see on that day, but I had another sensation and a memorable one. After dinner a little group, composed mainly of naval and military officers on embarkation duty, was established round the smoke-room fire in the South Western Hotel. We were all talking about the war, and all wishing that we were out in the thick of it. In the midst of this chorus of aspiration a telegram was handed to me inviting me to go to South Africa as a war correspondent for the *Manchester Guardian*. The chorus continued while I read, but it sounded far away; I was trying to realise what acquiescence in the request contained on the pink paper might mean. When I had decided I handed the telegram to my neighbour, and in a moment it had made the circuit of the group, trailing exclamations in its wake and changing the melancholy chorus to one of whole-hearted envy. I went to bed in some doubt as to whether I had received congratulations or condolences. In a few hours I was on my way to London; in a few days the flying wheels had carried me back to Southampton; but I thought that the busy docks wore a different face.

PART II

In the Wake of the Army

CHAPTER IV

The Long Sea Road

In the terms of the street, you make for Madeira from the Needles as straight as Ushant and Finisterre will permit, keep to the left until you catch the flare of the solitary light on Cape Verde, go on past that for about ten days, and Cape Town is the last place on the left. In the terms of the sea, your course is west-south-west until the Bay is open, then south-south-west, then south, and then south by east a half-east for the long stretch. But for most of us the way to the war lay through a stranger region than that. Years ago (as it seems) on a rainy winter evening, we watched the buoys of the Solent Channel streaming past us all aslope on the strong ebb-tide, and as the Trinity Brothers began to open their eyes for an all-night watch on the south coast, we closed ours to the world behind.

A day and night of dust and tumble in the Bay, and we awoke on a summer morning to find the wind blowing softly through the open ports and the water chiming on the ship's side. After that we lived in a world all our own; ourselves the sum and centre of it; a blue world that slid through degrees of latitude and longitude, but held us, its inhabitants, at ever the same distance from realities. The past was miles away at the end of the white path astern; the future did not yet so much as smudge the forward horizon; we were adrift, lost in the present.

Since we were, for the most part, Englishmen, we played games. At first we had walked about eyeing one another mistrustfully; but Time, the surest of teachers, soon convinced us of the essential harmlessness of our fellows. And then we played quoits, and danced and listened to the band, forgetting the things which were behind and disregarding (for the moment) the things which were before. Disregarding, but not quite forgetting. When the last game was over and the last pipe lighted, and the good, cool hours drew on, men used to sit in little groups watching the flash of waves tripping and spilling over smooth black furrows; and then they talked. The C.I.V. officers talked of Lee-Enfields, trajectories, mass and volley firing; the Indian Staff Corps men, who were going out on special service, spoke of commissariat and transport, of standing patrols and Cossack posts, of bivouacks, entrenchments, vedettes, contact squadrons, tactical sub-units, demolitions and entanglements. In those dark hours, while alien stars were rising and swinging westward over the masthead, hard, fit, clear-headed young men talked coolly and with common sense of the big business before them. The evening consultations were all that we gave to the future. The past was even less openly recognised; but it proclaimed itself eloquently in the withered bunches of flowers on this and that cabin table, in the demand for the ship's notepaper, in the women's trinkets worn by men who, under ordinary circumstances, would rather wear sack-cloth than jewellery: emblems, all of them, of thoughts that travelled the white road between the rudder and the horizon.

In that strange detached world of ours, energy alone was unsuspended. It was even stimulated, and in a race and class of men not accustomed to look inward for recreative resources manifested itself in a violent and unresting pursuit of artificial amusements. In this pursuit all our days were passed. The morning sun streams into the port-cabins, the diligent quartermaster brings our toys on deck and gravely arranges them; throughout the day we play with them until we are tired, when they are flung aside untidily; again the quartermaster returns, and, like a kind nurse, puts them away. The sun slants through the starboard windows and is quenched in the waters; a little talking, a little dancing, a little music, and we are all asleep. Such were our days. And ever before, behind, around and beneath us the moving, mysterious sea, wrinkled and old as the world, but blowing airs of eternal youth from its crumbling ridges. Down below iron floors stokers and trimmers were sweating, engineers were watching and nursing and feeding the great steel bondagers that drove us along; but how many of the light-hearted passengers ever thought of them? They were out of sight and mind, hidden away in their stifling holes, where in their relation to us they completed the satire of our miniature society.

I might give you a dozen pictures of our life, and yet mislead you as to its uncommonness; it was really commonplace life in strange and unfamiliar circumstances. Here is an example. At the first concert it was noticed, not without surprise, that the Captain's name was down for a song. Now for days the Captain had tramped alone up and down the deck – a large man, with a heavy face and drooping eye, and a head set forward on the shoulders by reason of long hours of staring into the sea dust; a man past middle-age, silent and (as we thought) surly. Therefore something like a sensation was produced when it was announced that the Captain would sing "Mary." I think I see and hear it now. The saloon filled with people; the windows framing faces of deck hands and firemen, with a background of moving blue; the heavy central figure, the kindly (we saw that now) Scotch face; the worn voice, unused to sustained utterance, gasping for breath in the middle of a line, and sometimes failing to be ready in time ("I lost the run of it," he explained to us in the middle of a temporary breakdown); the quaint simplicity of the words, "Kind, kind and gentle is she, kind is ma Ma-ary"; the thunder of applause that greeted the close; the immediate and unassailable popularity of the Captain. If I have described it as I saw it, you will understand why I shall always like to remember that scene. Here is another glimpse.

On a Sunday, when the church bells at home were jangling and the streets were (for a guess) streaming with rain and mud, it was Sunday with us also, three thousand miles away. The sun was lighting the lazy sea until it shone like a big blue diamond, the whales were spouting, the porpoises plunging and blowing, and here and there a shark lay basking near the surface with a wicked, wriggling, black fin exposed. It was very hot and still; the great sea people seemed to be revelling in some sort of Sabbath of their own, and the waters lay quiet and shining under the eye of Heaven. Here and there a drove of small flying-fishes rose and skimmed over the surface like swallows, but they too soon plunged into the blue and sought below that the cool green depths. Into this tranquil scene steamed the *Kinfauns Castle* in a triangle of snow, a big porpoise rolling and rollicking along beside her, now rising on this side, now on that. When he came very close he could see into the saloon windows, and presently he saw the Captain standing at the end of a table spread with the Union Jack and a great crowd of people sitting round the tables.

"Dearly beloved brethren," began the Captain, and then the porpoise's tail came up and his head went down with a "pflough!"

When he came up again near enough to see, all the people were muttering and gobbling over the Psalms, the Captain rolling out his short alternate verses as though he were directing his own quartermaster on a course. While the porpoise was very close to the ship and listening hard the ash-shoot was emptied almost on his head, which scared him so badly that he dived deep, and did not come up again for a long time. When he did rise the people were singing, "On, then, Christian soldiers, on to victory"; again he dived, and again came up with a snort, to hear them singing with equal vigour, "Make wars to cease and give us peace." But just then the third engineer opened the exhaust of the waste condenser water, and my black friend got such a shock when the cloud of steam and hot water burst from the ship's side that he altered his course three points, and I saw him plunging and rolling away to the west of south. One thing the porpoise did not hear, for he was below at the time. In his course through the Liturgy the Captain had reached the Collect for the day. I will warrant he was trained in a sterner school of theology than the Anglican; his voice and tones were never meant for the smooth diction of the Prayer-book; but that is neither here nor there. The "Coallect for the fourth Sunday after 'Pithany" rolled from his tongue. I never hope to hear it in a more appropriate time or place; there was something almost startling in the coincidence that brought it round on such a day, and there was significance in the words – "*O God, Who knowest us to be set in the midst of so many and great dangers that by reason of the frailty of our nature we cannot always stand upright; grant to us such strength and protection as may support us in all dangers and carry us through, all temptations.*" Thus prayed the Captain, the Chief Officer standing beside him; and none knew so well as those two how many and great were the dangers that lurked in our smiling environment.

As we drew nearer to our journey's end the desire for news became acute. At Madeira, on the 24th of January, we heard that the situation in Natal was practically unchanged, and up to February 3rd we had not seen another ship pass nearer than five miles. But then it was thought probable that we should meet the *Dunottar Castle* on her way home, and a bright look-out was kept. In the afternoon I was up on the bridge discussing celestial angles with the Chief Officer; we were snoring into the south-east trade, and the strong sun-warmed wind was a thing to bathe in; the bridge binoculars diligently swept the sharp blue line of horizon. Presently the Third Officer put his glass down. "There she is," said he, "two points on the starboard bow." We all looked, and we saw the tiny smear of smoke on the line. How strange it was; both of us coming up from nowhere and meeting on this roadless waste! In a quarter of an hour we raised her masts and funnel, and then we perceived it was not the *Dunottar*. Our course was altered two points, and the three of us stood up there in the wind and sun watching the growing speck. Down below they had just seen her, and glasses were levelled by the hundred. In a little while we could see a red cross on her bow, and we made her out to be a hospital ship carrying home wounded – Buller's wounded, we said, from the Tugela fight.

"BWF, HLF, WBQ," fluttered out our signal flags in a bravery of scarlet and blue and white, which is, being interpreted, "What news since the 24th?"

She was abeam now, a mile away; how slow they were in running up an answer! We pictured their signal quartermaster racking the pigeon-holes to spell "Ladysmith," and expected a gaudy display. Presently the coloured stream blew out from her main topmast stay. Only four flags!

"DFPC," reported the Third Officer, and there was a scramble for the Code-book. "Nothing important since last accounts."

Could anything be more exasperating? We ran up another question, I do not know what, but we waited in vain for the answering flutter, and the hospital ship *Princess of Wales* rolled along on the blue swell.

"South by east-a-half-east," snapped the Chief Officer; the wheel spun and the steering engine hissed, and the *Kinfauns Castle* drove her stem into it again, while from the promenade deck rose the sound of many voices.

And so we went driving along again through a wonderful sea of deep blue rollers jousting on a grey ground. It did not yet appear where we should go or what would be our lot; to-night or to-morrow we should know; but to-day it was enough that the sun shone and that the waters were wide.

CHAPTER V

Scenes at Cape Town

When at last the *Kinfauns Castle* carried us on a sunny evening out of blue emptiness into Cape Town harbour and dumped us down on dry land, about thirty of us who were on our way to the front took elaborate farewells – only to meet again twelve hours later in the vestibule at headquarters.

No one was in the least excited by our arrival. If we were special service men, we were told that there were no instructions for us, and that we had better turn up three or four times a day and look at the order-board. If we were correspondents, heads were shaken, and smooth-spoken people with stars and crowns on their shoulder-straps said they doubted very much whether Lord Roberts would grant any more passes. If we were nobodies who had come out (with more or less direct encouragement from the officials) in the hope of getting commissions, we were turned away like tramps, and told that there was "nothing for us." It was all rather flattening and dispiriting.

When we turned up again at headquarters next morning we found the place empty but for a Kaffir charwoman snuffling over her brushes: Lord Roberts gone, Lord Kitchener gone, all the staff gone, stolen away like thieves in the night, gone "to the front." No one was left in authority, no one knew anything about us; so we went to the barracks and worried irresponsible officers who would have moved heaven and earth for us if they could, but they "had no instructions." At last, in a remote corner of the barrack buildings, someone discovered a major who was in charge of the Intelligence Department. Didn't we all fall upon him like birds of prey! In half an hour the telegraph that connected Cape Town with the Commander-in-Chief was thrilling all our wants northward; in six hours half the special service men were flying about the town collecting sardines and whisky and ink; in twenty-four hours only a few of us were left, still worrying the unfortunate major. Then the wires began to come back from Lord Roberts saying that no licence must be granted to this man and that; that there were more than enough correspondents at the front; and at this news some of us began to quake. At this critical point, when I was wandering in the corridor of the post office, I found the Press Censor, all alone and unguarded; so I fastened upon him and drove him, the kindest and most amiable of men, into his office, and stood over him while he wrote a long telegram to the chief, in which many reasons were given why I should go to the front. The result was that I received the desired privilege, but when I left Cape Town many men were still haunting the barracks and the post office.

My week of waiting was a busy time, but in the intervals between sitting down before staff officers, interviewing possible – and impossible – servants, and trying horses, I contrived to see a little of the Cape Town life in those martial days.

One seemed to be no nearer the war there than in London or Manchester. Troops marched to the station and disappeared into the night; so they did at home. There were hospitals there, filled with wounded men; none so large or so full as Netley. There was a big camp there; not so big a camp as Aldershot. And the place was full of officers, coming and going, even as Southampton had been crowded with officers pausing on their way to or from the war. Then there was at Cape Town something like a famine of news; by far the latest and most trustworthy came from London. Things that thrilled us out there and were cabled home in hot haste were found to be stale news in England. As the storm blows over the cliff far out to sea, but leaves the hamlet on the shore in absolute peace, so Cape Town seemed to be sheltered by the big, dominating mountain from all the home-going news, and to abide in peaceful ignorance while the telegraph-rooms resounded to the talk of the needles.

I rather dreaded the hospitals, but they were magnificent. To see so many men bearing pain bravely and cheerfully were privilege enough; but to find men who had undergone the most dreadful tortures soberly begging and hoping to be sent back to the front showed one what can be accomplished by discipline and an ideal of conduct. Here is an example. Two men lay side by side in the Wynberg hospital. One had five holes in his body, made during a charge by as many bullets. He had nearly recovered. The other had been shot while lying down, and the bullet had passed along his back and touched the base of his spine, paralysing him for ever. Both men were almost weeping; the first with joy because there was a chance of his returning to the front, the second with grief because he was powerless to help his comrades any more. I could cite a hundred examples of the astounding spirit that such men displayed. I do not think that we at home ever doubted their bravery on the field, but the kind of endurance that is seldom bred but by long habit and early training was to be found no less universally in these hospital beds. The people of Cape Town had done well in the matter of hospitals, and fully half the accommodation was provided by public subscription. But

Government hospitals were far from efficient in their equipment, as well as far from sufficient in their accommodation. Many things that would be regarded as necessaries in a pauper hospital at home had to be provided at Cape Town for the Government hospitals by private bounty.

I walked over to the infantry camp at Sea Point one morning with Mr. Rudyard Kipling. As we neared the camp we overtook a private carrying in his hand a large pair of boots. Mr. Rudyard Kipling asked if we were on the right road, and the man said –

"Yes; are yer goin' there? Then yer can tike these boots. I 'av to entrine at twelve o'clock, and I ain't goin' ter miss it fer no blessed boots. 'Ere, tike 'old," he continued, thrusting the boots into Mr. Kipling's hand, "and give 'em to Private Dickson, B Company; and mind, if yer cawn't find 'im, jest tike 'em back ter Williams, opposite the White 'Orse."

Mr. Kipling promised faithfully, and gave a receipt, which he signed; but the man did not notice the name.

"My friend," said Mr. Kipling, "you'll get your head chaffed off when you get back to the guard-room."

"What for?" vainly asked the man, and departed, while we continued our way towards the camp.

No sooner were we inside the railings than Mr. Kipling was accosted by a military policeman.

"What are you doing here? You must get out of here, you know, sharp!"

"I'm taking these boots to Private Dickson," said Mr. Kipling.

"Well, you ought to take them to the guard tent, and not go wandering about the camp like this. Out of it, now!"

Now Mr. Kipling had a pass from the Commander-in-Chief to go wherever he pleased in South Africa, and, besides that, he is Rudyard Kipling, whom private soldiers call their brother and father; so the situation was amusing.

Just then a police sergeant rode up and said, "Please, sir, I lived ten years with the man as you get your tobacco from in Brighton; anything I can do for you?"

"Yes," said Mr. Kipling, "I want this man taken away and killed!"

The youth was much confused, but he had done his duty; so Private Dickson had his boots, and great was the mirth and loud the cheering about the tents of B Company.

This police protection of the camps was surprisingly close, but one learned the reason when one had moved about for a little while among the military authorities. For here, even in the heart of British territory, the Boer spy was feared; he was thought to be the servant of an agency hardly less invisible and powerful than the Open Eye of the Mormons; and one was told that his machinations were as patent as his secrecy was perfect. One morning a section of the railings surrounding picketed horses would be found demolished; on another the whole milk supply of a camp would be infected by some poisonous bacillus. It seems almost incredible, but it is true that all such mishaps were attributed to Boer treachery. In the popular imagination the Boer agent moved undiscovered amid the daily life of Cape Town; at noon in the busy street; in the club smoke-room; in the hotel dining-room – a woman this time, arrayed in frocks from Paris, and keeping a table charmed by her conversation. And yet the objects of this superstitious dread were allowed to have qualities that made some of our officers dislike their business. An English officer said to me one night:

"One can't say it here without being misunderstood, but I love the Boers, even though I am fighting them. My father was a colonist, and these men were like brothers of his. I have been in houses here where I knew there were guns stored for the enemy, and where the sons would probably be fighting me in the field, and the people have almost cried when I have been going away; neither of us talked about it, but each knew what was in the other's mind. People say they're like animals, and perhaps they are; at least they're like animals in this, that once you make them distrust you, you'll never win their confidence again. And they don't trust us."

That officer is well enough known, and universally admired as a smart soldier; but not everyone who sees the keen soldier, anxious above all things for his own country's success, realises with what conflicting emotions he goes to the fight.

I was anxious to see a real live Boer, as I thought it quite improbable that I should see one at the front; half the officers and men who had been wounded had never seen one of the enemy. So, having heard that our Boer prisoners – 450 in number – had been landed from Her

Majesty's ship *Penelope* and encamped at Simonstown, I went there to visit them.

From Cape Town the land stretches an arm southward to the Cape of Good Hope and Bellows Rock, where it divides the Atlantic from the Indian Ocean. The mainland runs about as far southward, so that the arm partly encloses the waters of False Bay; and in the hollow of its elbow nestles Simonstown. This is a cluster of white houses on the sea-beat foot of a hill that sweeps upward to the giddy white clouds. All day long at that season the hill is steeped in sunshine; all day long its lower slopes reverberate to the assault of the rollers while the summit is folded in the silence of the upper air. Close in-shore half a dozen cruisers were lying like rocks among the deep moving waters; the St. George's ensign floated from the shore flagstaffs, and an air of whiteness and tidiness proclaimed the naval station.

The railway from Cape Town runs so close to the shore of the bay that you cannot hear yourself speak for the noise of bursting surf. It brought me to Simonstown in the full glare and heat of the afternoon. The prisoners were encamped about a hundred yards out of the town, and as we walked through the street we spoke with pity of men imprisoned on such a day. What we expected I do not quite know – dungeons perhaps, or cells hewn out of the rock – but it was with something like a shock of disappointment or relief (according to our notions of appropriate treatment for prisoners) that we caught our first view of the encampment. Just beyond the town the hillside takes a gentler slope, dipping a lawn of sea-grass into the water; and it was upon this charming spot, enclosed with a double fence, that the prisoners were quartered. We pressed our faces against the wires and stared, much as one stares in the Zoo at a cageful of newly-arrived animals that have cost a great deal of money and maybe a life or two. Fine, big men, stalwart and burned brown by the sun; stern-looking, but with that air of large contentment they wear who live much alone and out of doors; massive of jaw and forehead, moulded after a grand pattern. They were lying on the grass, standing in little groups, sauntering up and down in the hot sunshine, playing cricket with ponderous energy, bathing and sporting in the clear apple-green water. It was not their contentment that surprised me, but the perfection of their circumstances. They were encamped on such a spot as people pay large sums for the privilege of pitching tents upon; they were numerous enough to make themselves independent of alien company; the sun was shining, the sea breeze blowing; they had food and drink, and tobacco to smoke; where they bathed an eight-oar gig from the *Powerful* swung on the swell, not so much to prevent escape as to render assistance to tired swimmers.

So our prisoners blinked in the sun and listened to the organ-note of the surf, and brooded on the most beautiful picture I have ever seen: masses of bare rock towering into the bright sky, and an endless pageant of seas rolling grandly homeward from the south, from the infinite purple and blue of the Indian Ocean, grounding at the edge of the green lawn and showering snow upon the hot rocks.

CHAPTER VI

In the eddies of a great whirl

When I arrived at Modder River Camp, on February 17th, the guns were being hauled back from the hills into camp, tents were being struck, and waggon transport organised. The plain was a cloud of hot, whirling sand that shrouded near objects as closely as a fog, but, instead of the damp coldness of a fog, the plain was radiating heat that sent the thermometer inside one's tent up to 135 degrees. The place that a few days before had been resounding with artillery was now silent and (by comparison) deserted; buck waggons took the place of gun carriages, and the ambulance cart carried mails from home. One thought of Modder River as being surely at "the front," but here was the place, here were the troops, the guns, the hospitals, the sand-enveloped cemetery, and yet one seemed to be no nearer than before to actual war. As for news, there was less even than at Cape Town. A few telegrams, days old, fluttered from the notice-board, and in at headquarters I found that we who had been sixty hours on the journey from Cape Town were hailed as newsbearers. There was a press censor, yet one could not send press telegrams; headquarters had moved on to Jacobsdaal; telegrams must go through headquarters, and the wire to Jacobsdaal was only to be used for military purposes. This was something like a block, so Mr. Amery, of the *Times*, and I, resolved to ride over to Jacobsdaal and see if we could get any news.

We crossed the Riet and Modder drifts, and passed over the island where the shells and bullets had been singing so shrilly on the day of the big fight. When we passed the birds were singing instead, sending down with the cooing pigeons a chorus from the trees. No one could tell us whether or not the twelve miles to Jacobsdaal were free from the enemy; people thought so, but they were not quite sure. So we rode along, observing the dry veldt not without interest, but the lonely road heaved up and down over the plain and revealed little sign of human occupation. Once we passed a convoy carrying stores to the front, and at about the eighth mile a little Boer camp of about a dozen tents, all deserted, and apparently in haste, for there were half-emptied tins of provisions and a few cooking utensils scattered about, and a dead horse lay by the roadside. The heat was very great, and was only supportable when one kept a drenched handkerchief under one's hat. Indeed, officers who had come straight out from India protested that they never felt there anything like the heat of that South African drought.

Jacobsdaal, a little white town or village near the river, appeared at last from a ridge of the plain. It contained an inn, and the inn contained cups of tea – a fact in connection with Jacobsdaal that I shall long remember. In about an hour we were ready to look about a little, but at headquarters we could only learn that the front had again moved forward. We could not advance without transport, and we could get no quarters, so we lay down in a stony field under the stars, and made a poor shift at sleeping through a concert of complaining oxen and cocks cheering all night long, with an undertone of rumbling wheels on the distant road.

Next morning early I rode back to Modder, where I collected with difficulty two sorry but useful nags and a Cape cart. On my way out I passed a sentry, who brought me up with the usual cry, "Halt! who goes there?"

"Friend," said I.

"Advance, friend, and give the countersign."

Now I did not know the countersign, and I had to tell him so. The private soldier is sometimes zealous and often stupid, and occasionally both; and in the pause that followed my answer I heard the click of his rifle. In that second of time I remembered a story which I had heard the day before of a sentry at Modder, who, when the guard came up in the dark to relieve him, made the usual challenge. "It's only us, old man," said the sergeant. "None of your blooming us," said the sentry, and shot the sergeant dead.

However the sentry was soon persuaded, and when I passed the outpost, the sentry who should really have stopped me and examined my passport treated me as a field-officer and presented arms, so I rode away back to the dust of Modder. There I collected as much forage as possible, and the next day rode back with my caravan to Jacobsdaal. Once more there was a block. The front forty miles away; no more forage, no rations even; and I starved officially, but was entertained privately by the commandant. The front was reaching away forward along the road to Bloemfontein; and as telegrams had to be censored there and handed in at Modder River, fifty miles away, and as I had no despatch riders, I decided that the game was up on this line. A dose of fever helped my decision, and held me afterwards at Modder when great things were happening at Paardeberg. But for the day during which I stayed in Jacobsdaal I studied the little town and its alien inhabitants.

Jacobsdaal stands four-square on the northern bank of the Riet River, eleven miles east-south-east from Modder; and the manner of its occupation, as described to me by General Wavell (who captured it on the 15th of February and remained in it as commandant), seems to have been surprisingly neat and effectual. General Chermside, commanding the 14th Brigade, left Enslin on the 11th and marched to Ramdam, where he was joined by General Wavell, commanding the 15th Brigade, who had moved from Graspan. From Ramdam the two brigades marched almost due east to Dekiel's Drift, which they were delayed in crossing during the whole of the 13th. They started again on the next evening and made a night march to Wegdraai, where they arrived at four o'clock on the morning of the 15th. An officer of the North Staffordshire Regiment told me that he never saw anything so impressive as that night march. The horizon was level all round like the sea, and all night long it was alive with streams of lightning that lighted up the plain with the brigade crawling across it through the thunder. On the 15th General Wavell's brigade was detached, and at midday started to march upon Jacobsdaal. The brigade was strengthened by about seventy men of the C.I.V. (who acted as scouts) and by a battery of artillery. The North Staffordshires acted as advance guard, the South Wales Borderers and the Cheshire Regiment formed the main body, and the East Lancashires brought up the rear – half a battalion as reserves and half as rear-guard with the baggage.

The position was an admirable one for the enemy. General Wavell had the town ahead and the river on the left parallel with his line of march; and as he approached, the Boers (about 400 strong) opened a brisk fire on his flank from the river-bed. The fire was directed at the C.I.V.'s, who were advancing on the right bank of the river; but it had a double objective, since what missed the C.I.V.'s had a fair chance of finding the Staffordshires, who were advancing on a parallel ridge still further to the right. The C.I.V.'s had a good many horses killed, and many of the men were wounded and "dropped," but I believe only one was killed. Finding the attack was coming from the left, the General showed his force on that side, at the same time shelling the south-east corner of the town. He would do no more because of the women and children in the place; and, considering his disadvantage, the Boers with a little more determination might have held the town. After showing on the left General Wavell swept round on the right, sending the North Staffordshires towards the north side. There they entered, and the place was, so to speak, nipped between the two arms of the brigade, with the artillery in the middle ready to speak. The Boers now broke and fled south-west and north-west, followed by showers of shrapnel. "It was an awfully pretty sight," the General remarked to me, "to see the shrapnel bursting all round in showers; one of the prettiest things I have ever seen." The enemy had open country and soon got away, but in the meantime the Union Jack was blowing bravely over Jacobsdaal, and we were in possession of a most important square on the big chessboard of the Orange Free State.

Of course the chief importance of the position was that it formed a depôt for stores and a halting-place for convoys on the way to the front. The General, with Captain Carleton (brigade-major) and Captain Davidson (A.D.C.), was under fire during the whole of this brisk little action; and Captain Carleton told me that the bullets were whizzing past as briskly at two thousand yards as at two hundred. It need hardly be said that since there were only three staff-officers, whose lives were of the utmost value to the expedition, they spent most of their time in and about the front firing lines. As soon as the General had occupied the square he turned his men out and bivouacked them on the plain round the village. They were exhausted after an eight-mile march, with this action at the end of it; hot and thirsty too, suffering from such heat and thirst as is only known in dusty deserts like the Karoo in time of drought. There was a certain amount of looting – chiefly of cloth and stuffs from the shops; but it was suddenly brought to an end by Lord Roberts's startling order that any man found in the act of looting, or any man against whom acts of looting could be proved, would be hanged, and his battalion sent down to the base. There was no more looting. "There *were* three ducks found with their necks wrung," the General admitted, "but we paid for them!"

The occupation of Jacobsdaal was, of course, only an incident in the great whirl of operations which began on the 3rd of February, when General Macdonald with the Highland Brigade moved westward from Modder River and seized Koodoesberg. Hitherto we had been waging a very straightforward kind of war, and Lord Roberts's masterly tactics between Modder River and Paardeberg were the first hint we had given our enemy that we also could be cunning. When I arrived at Modder River the wheels of this great operation were spinning, but Modder itself was in an eddy, where there was no movement and little news of any. French was racing to head Cronje off on the north of the Modder River, and the main body of the army was advancing in his rear, but we at Modder River knew next to nothing of these movements.

It is worth while to recall the principal events in Lord Roberts's operations near Modder River. The seizing of Koodoesberg was, of course, intended to divert the attention of the Boers from the points at which the real movement was taking place. On the 8th of the month

General Macdonald was recalled to Modder River; on the 9th Lord Roberts arrived there and assumed command; on the 12th General French marched from Ramdam, where he had been collecting a big cavalry force, seized Dekiel's Drift and Klip Drift on the Modder, and the next day occupied a commanding position on the north of the river, capturing three of the enemy's laagers. On the 15th, having traversed Cronje's communications, French reached Kimberley and dislodged the enemy from the southern side of the town; they evacuated Magersfontein and Spytfontein, and retreated to Koodoesrand, contriving in their turn to slip through our containing lines. Jacobsdaal was captured on the same day, and on the 16th of February began the fighting at Paardeberg, which was only brought to an end by Cronje's surrender on the 27th.

However, one was only (as I have said) in the stagnant middle of things at Jacobsdaal, and the outer currents did not reach us. From our point of view Jacobsdaal was not an important station on the war-path to Bloemfontein; it was simply a place of insufficient food, bad smells, choking dust, and many hospitals. The Red Cross flag flew from all the churches and every available house; furniture was piled in verandahs, and pews were stacked in churchyards.

Enteric was rife there; but could a man, officer or private, who had been out for twelve hours on foraging or convoy duty, sit down and boil his water and then wait for a drink until it cooled? Because the water looked clear and innocent they drank it by the quart, and therefore the hospitals were full. Jacobsdaal is responsible for many of the inglorious deaths of "active service."

Early one morning, while the air was yet fresh and cool, General Wavell took me round with him on his hospital inspection. He is one of the small, keen, kind-eyed men who emerge in the senior ranks of the army. One never meets them as subalterns, and they represent the army's best workmanship in the matter of moulding and finishing. We were still talking about the "pretty" little action when we entered the first hospital – a small Dutch church. I should have said that besides our own field hospitals at Jacobsdaal there was a Boer hospital and one of the German Red Cross Society.

This first was the Boer hospital, and even at this early hour the air was pungent with the reek of strong tobacco. The General spoke to all the patients, and had a kind word for everyone, and they all greeted him with gratitude and cordiality. Their one cry was, "We've had as much as we want. If we could only get back to our farms!" Most of those to whom I spoke said that they had never wanted to fight us, never hoped to beat us, and were heartily sick of the whole affair. "I wish I could send you back to your homes, men," said the General; "but I must obey orders." They chatted away to us, and said they hoped the General would come in often. It was much the same in the German and English houses, only here Boers and Englishmen lay side by side, sharing pipes and papers and talk with each other. Truly, animosity ceases at the hospital door; and the attitude of these men who had been menacing each other's lives and now lay stricken together was not unlike the shame-faced amity of children who have been caught fighting, and are made to share a punishment.

And no one was more concerned and depressed by the whole business than the brisk little General, who had been speaking almost caressingly of his shells and shrapnel. He is surely a good soldier who fights at as small a cost as possible, disregards that cost while he fights, and afterwards so behaves that his enemies like to take him by the hand.

Hospitals, where so many virtues too tender for the airs of the outside world have time to bloom, are generally attractive rather than repulsive places, and I was on that account the more surprised to find myself repelled by these field-hospitals. To see men lying about distorted, impotent, disfigured by all kinds of fantastic deformities, their wounds still new, themselves lying near the spot where they fell; and to remember the cause of it all, and how vague that cause really was to the men who were suffering for it; the grossness and brutality of mutilation – here a man with lead in his bowels, there a man with his face obliterated, one man groaning and spitting from bleeding lungs, another, struck by a great piece of flying iron, silent under the shock of news that his sight was gone for ever; the feeling that these men were suffering on our account, and the realisation that every one of us has had his share in the responsibility for the whole, makes a load that one cannot, or should not, slough away in a moment.

CHAPTER VII

Magersfontein and Kimberley

There was a train going to Kimberley with cattle and forage on the afternoon of Thursday, February 22nd, and the stagnation of everything except dust at Modder being complete, I jumped on the twenty-ninth truck as the engine was taking up the slack of the couplings and was immediately jerked forward on the newly-mended road to the north. I had nothing with me except what I stood in and a waterproof; but as the journey of twenty-four miles occupied four hours, and as the heavens poured down a deluge during three hours and twenty-five minutes of the time I was glad to have even that. The line passes beside Magersfontein and through gaps in six ridges behind it, affording an excellent view of the whole position. That position seemed to me practically impregnable. To have won a way to Kimberley upon this road would probably have meant six bloody battles, always with the likelihood of a reverse after each for the attacking army. Imagine a wide and perfectly level plain with a ridge standing straight across it like a great railway embankment, but with arms at each end curving towards the front as the arms of a trench are curved; behind the ridge, and higher, two or three kopjes which command it; behind the kopjes another ridge like the first, with more kopjes to command it; the same thing repeated half a dozen times, without another eminence within fifteen miles. Imagine this, and you see the country between Modder River and Kimberley. And throughout the position every piece of open ground was slashed and seamed by trenches and works, constructed as though for the inspection of an examiner in engineering – beautiful, artistic, formidable work that filled the mind of every British officer who saw it with envy and admiration. Behind the hills were little huts and hiding-places contrived within the shadow of the low, thick trees that grow there, so that not a soul lived out of cover. Captain Austin, R.A., who shared the humidity of my truck, and who had been in charge of a 6-inch field-gun trained on Magersfontein at eight thousand yards, told me that he could see through his glasses the whole working of the enemy's admirable system. They had a look-out man sitting at the far end of a long tunnel of rock and stone; when we fired he gave the signal, and the Boers got into cover; and twenty seconds afterwards, when our shell, beautifully aimed and timed, arrived on the hill, it spent itself upon the flinty rock. Then the Boers showed their heads and fired; and their shell swept through its arc and exploded, generally finding its mark.

The battle of Magersfontein has been the subject of more prolonged discussion than any other single event in the war. Coming on the day after our reverse at Stormberg, it completed the momentary demoralisation of a great mass of people at home who had expected the campaign to resolve itself into a sweeping march on Pretoria. Like the affair of Majuba, it has been sentimentally magnified out of all proportion to its military importance. On the strength of the emotions roused by our disaster, thousands graduated as military critics and cried aloud for the recall of Lord Methuen. Private soldiers with shattered nerves wrote home hysterical narratives and criticisms which were published and commented upon, and treated as valuable evidence. We lost our heads for the moment; there is no doubt of that; but people who are thus betrayed into panic will not be appeased until they have made a scapegoat of someone. Lord Methuen was, of course, the obvious sacrifice. Why did he make a frontal attack? Why did he fail?

It is well to remember that Lord Methuen was being pressed to relieve Kimberley, which represented its case as extreme. He must do something. Naturally he designed the kind of attack which the forces at his disposal were best suited to deliver. A long turning movement was out of the question since he had not the mounted men for it. As for the "frontal attack" at Magersfontein, of which we have heard so much, Lord Methuen never designed and did not deliver a direct frontal attack. His plan was to surprise the extreme left of Cronje's position, and at the same time contain the whole of his front with a strong force. And no competent critic has ventured to suggest any better disposal of the forces then available for the purposes of attack. No, Lord Methuen has not been criticised and abused because he used his force in one way rather than in another, but simply because he failed.

There is very often more to be learned from a failure than a success, and this particular failure is worthy of a little study. Everyone knows that the reason why the attack on Magersfontein failed was, first, because the Highland Brigade lost its way and came unexpectedly into contact with the enemy's position, and, secondly, because they failed to rally after the first confusion, when (in the opinion of many experts who were present) a little confidence would probably have saved the day. If any single precaution was neglected, if any pains were spared in the reconnoitring of the position or in securing the proper conduct of the troops towards the place from which their attack was to be delivered, then Lord Methuen was absolutely to blame. But the more that is known about this unfortunate affair the more clearly it will be seen that Lord Methuen neglected no precaution and spared no pains. The rain and pitch darkness were the act of God, and no general in the world can prevail when Nature is so completely in league with the enemy as she was on the night of Magersfontein.

I do not care to dwell on the malice and cruel unfairness of many of the attacks on Lord Methuen, because, for my country's sake, I hope they will soon be forgotten; but if anyone should still suppose that these great hysterical waves of public feeling select their victims impartially, I would ask him to compare the battle of Magersfontein with the fruitless attack delivered by Lord Kitchener on the Paardeberg laager on February 18th. In one case time was working against Lord Methuen, and threatening to exhaust the endurance of Kimberley; in the other case time was working with Lord Kitchener, limiting the resistance of Cronje to a calculable number of days and hours. In one case there was a small force which, owing to the nature of its composition, could only be used in one way; in the other case there was a large and splendidly-assorted force, which gave opportunity for an infinite variety of combinations. In one case the attack was turned by circumstances which no human being could have prevented into a frontal contact; in the other case that form of attack was deliberately chosen. In one case the casualties were about nine hundred; in the other, about sixteen hundred. And in one case the general officer commanding has been insulted and attacked and defamed, while the officer responsible for the second affair is still regarded by the masses as a consummate master of field operations.

This is a long digression; I have made it here because the subject of it is inseparable from my memory of the dark and stony ranges which I saw closely for the first time through the pitiless rain of that February day. Miserable as the journey was, its passage through the country occupied so lately by the enemy made it interesting. The way in which our sappers had toiled to repair the line was beyond praise. Every telegraph post had been blasted in two pieces by dynamite; every culvert had been blown up; nearly every insulator smashed; the wires (about seven in number) had been cut every few hundred yards; yet within four days from the relief of Kimberley trains had begun to go up the whole distance and telegraphic communication had been restored. I saw the work that had been done, and the difficulty of it, and was proud of the way in which it was accomplished. Not that there is little to be proud of in the work of the army. On the contrary, one is amazed to see what is accomplished in spite of the system, amazed to find what can be done by able men against the most determined opposition from their own side; but the great fact that was brought out by the earlier part of this campaign is that the man of intelligence and initiative and ability and energy was fast in the clutches of the Red Tape spider, which fussed round him until he was enveloped in the scarlet web and impotent to use brains or energy. Engineering is one of the few things of which corporate bodies admit their ignorance; therefore the sappers got through much admirable work quietly and quickly.

The approach to Kimberley with its mine shafts and hills of blue dust reminded me of the Black Country. What one noticed first with regard to the town was the number of holes and shelters and warrens into which people had crept for safety. Hundreds of them, like human anthills; and one thought, What strange place is this, where men fear to walk upright? The menu at the principal hotel, where I dined, would (if it had been printed) have consisted of one item – horseflesh. I noticed that the residents ate it eagerly, and even talked about it; but most of us strangers arose hungry and went quickly into the fresh air.

That night and the next morning I walked through the town and talked to people who had been living there; and it was when I talked to the people that I began to realise what had been happening. The few ruined buildings and riddled walls conveyed little to me. But when one found man after man thin, listless, and (in spite of the joy of salvation) dispirited; talking with a tired voice and hopeless air, and with a queer, shifty, nervous, scared look in the eye, one began to understand.

The thing was scarcely human, scarcely of this world. These men were not like oneself. If you threaten an inexperienced boxer with a quick play of fists on every side of his head, even though you never touch him, you may completely demoralise him; he shies at every feint and every movement. And these people had been in a situation comparable with that of the poor boxer. Think of it. The signal from the conning tower, the clamour of bells and whistles, the sudden silence amongst the people, the rush for shelter, and then the hum and roar, like wind in a chimney, of the huge iron cylinder flying through the air, potent for death. And then, perhaps, the noise of a falling building, or the scream of some human creature who is nothing but a mass of offence when you come up five seconds later. Think of this repeated six or seven – sometimes sixty or seventy – times during the daylight hours, and can you wonder that men should lose their placid manners and scuttle like rats into their holes at the dreaded sound? And all this fear and horror to be borne upon an empty stomach, for the horrors of partial starvation were added to the constant fear of a violent death. Mothers had to see their babies die because there was no milk or other suitable nourishment; a baby cannot live on horse and mule flesh. There was hardly a coloured baby left alive; and that one statement accounts for whole lifetimes of misery and suffering.

It was not until the Boers had mounted their 6-inch gun on the 8th of February that the panic began. People had got used to the smaller shells, which could often be dodged; besides, the enemy did not fire so many of them. But when the big gun began its seventy rounds a day people lost their self-command and began to dig and scratch in the earth for shelter. Thousands went down the mines and sat all day in the bowels of the earth. Men walking in the streets jumped if a mule kicked an iron plate; they screamed when the signal was given; they broke and ran and burrowed into shelter. Yet so fast do some men anchor themselves to routine that many kept their offices open and did business – all the while, however, with one eye on the paper and the other glancing through the door or window; ever with one ear turned to the speaker and the other noting the rustle of paper stirred by the breeze and the hum of wind under the door.

That only twenty people were killed is no fact at all in connection with the panic; what really matters is that seventy times a day something happened which might have killed a dozen people.

I have only to add, in case I am accused of exaggerating the state of terror, that the people who went through this ordeal have not necessarily the clearest conception of it. I came out of the safe outer world and saw their faces and eyes, and, if I had not heard a word, I should have known.

One other thing. A despatch sent by me to *The Manchester Guardian* contained this sentence complimentary to the De Beers Company: "The condition of the town would have been deplorable but for the relief administration of the De Beers Company."

That sentence was not made, but suggested by my good friend the censor; and it will serve to indicate how great was the bowing down before the house of De Beers. I wish to disavow any compliment I may have appeared to pay that company in my telegram, for I think they did their bare duty. What they did was to provide a ration of soup for the inhabitants as long as some bullock meat which they possessed lasted; to organise relief works by making roads and fences in a town which belongs chiefly to themselves; and to allow people to shelter in their mines. Perhaps they could do no more. Considering everything, and remembering some facts in connection with this and other political troubles, I ask, Could they well have done less?

CHAPTER VIII

Paardeberg

From Modder River to Paardeberg the road rolls over a bare yet beautiful plain, brown and dry before the rain, but after a heavy rain bursting into endless stretches of purple and scarlet flowers of the karoo. I went by Jacobsdaal. Early on Wednesday morning, February 28th, I rode out from the little town with General Wavell, who put me a couple of miles on the road. You are to understand that this was something of an adventure. I had nothing but a Cape cart and a couple of horses to draw it – a thing that holds, with one's kit, about three hundred pounds of forage. I was going to a camp where I could get no forage and hardly any food; there was not a despatch-rider to be had at Modder; my telegrams must be ridden back from the front, now thirty and soon to be ninety miles away. Sickness had tethered me to Modder River camp throughout the exciting week that had ended with Cronje's surrender; and now on February 28th I was following the army, feeling like one who should enter a theatre as the curtain was falling on the first act.

The thirty-mile ride through the lonely country would have been delightful but for the dismal trail left by the war – carcases of horses and oxen lining the road, a carcase every few hundred yards surrounded by a gorged flock of aasvögels, the foulest of the vulture tribe. With a nervous horse the passage of these pestilential spots was made difficult as well as revolting, and it was with a feeling of relief that one saw the tents and waggons of the Paardeberg camp by the river trees.

Along the road, I should have said, the trail was one of devastation. In the midst of the dry veldt one sometimes came upon a farmhouse with its grove of trees, and spring, and pleasant fields; but always the farm was derelict, windows broken, rooms gutted, stock destroyed, with often some poor abandoned creature tethered to a tree, and waiting, in the midst of the dead silence of the empty country, to be fed and watered.

At Paardeberg I found the headquarters camp situated on the river bank, a place pretty to look at but horrible to be near. The only water to drink was that from a well by the river – water of a dark and strange colour; and even while one drank it one sat and watched the carcases of horses floating down the brown stream from the deserted Boer laager a mile above. For Cronje and his men had surrendered, not only because of losses or lack of ammunition, but chiefly, it was said, because the same conditions that made our camp almost unbearable made his laager in the river-bed impossible for human accommodation. So he surrendered, after a resistance that will live in history as one of the bravest pieces of human endurance.

On my way down I had met a great company of men moving over the plain surrounded by mounted infantry. These were our prisoners – a noble bag of more than four thousand. But now that they had gone there was no reason why the camp should be maintained at Paardeberg, and at noon we proceeded to thread our way eastward – a long procession of men and horses and waggons – to the farm of Osfontein, where the force was being concentrated for the final advance. The delay was fortunate for the correspondents, for those of us who had only a scanty stock of provisions and forage could send our carts back once more to Modder for a supply. In the meantime nothing was likely to happen until a fortnight's stock of provisions and forage for the army had been collected.

Before leaving Paardeberg, and in the intervals of arranging the mere details of living – which on this line of advance were harassing and formidable – I rode over to the deserted Boer laager, or as near to it as was safe. The scene was strange and significant. Imagine the river, deep down between steep terraced banks, flowing through the level plain. On the left side our position, well entrenched, with a few kopjes about two thousand yards from the bank. On the right was the enemy's position, which extended further down the banks of the river and up to the very edge of our side. On the far bank I saw a line of hundreds of transport waggons and carts, all empty, many of them smashed and broken by our shell fire. But it was the river-bed itself that was most interesting. The water was very low, and there was any amount of cover on the steep banks, and this was increased by a number of small pits or trenches – not long trenches like ours, but simple little holes or graves dug in the banks, with room enough for a couple of men. Graves they proved to be in many cases, for where the Boers were shot in them the trenches were simply filled in and the bodies thus rudely buried. But how independent they were! No bulky commissariat department, no army of cooks and butchers – every man with his own kettle and biltong or canned beef, his own rug or sleeping bag, his own water-bottle; so that when he came into such a position as this he could remain in it for days together. One saw many pathetic things in these trenches – garments and personal belongings evidently made by hands that did not work for hire.

In two trenches I found Dutch Bibles; in one a diary of the last few weeks; in almost all some sign that human beings and not machines had been at work there; and on all sides spent shells and shrapnel cases and cartridges, to remind one of the nature of their work. When one followed, as I had followed so far, in the shadow of the war and not in the midst of it, in the track of the Red Cross and the wayside cemetery instead of within sound and sight of the thing itself, one saw a very dark and unrelieved side of it – the shadow without the substance, the effect without the cause.

PART III

Lord Roberts's Advance to Bloemfontein

CHAPTER IX

The Boer Panic at Osfontein

The carefully prepared attack of Lord Roberts on the Boer position at Osfontein was delivered on Wednesday, March 7th, with the result that the enemy fled without attempting to defend his extremely strong position. To understand the gravity of the attack you must have been there during the last few days of preparation, when hills and ridges, subsequently abandoned in a moment, were being strengthened and armed with trenches and guns. On Sunday and Monday, the 4th and 5th of March, I rode round the whole position, and, like everyone else, was led to expect a very severe struggle. The position was roughly this. The great plain through which the river winds is broken five miles east of Osfontein by a long range of kopjes extending about fourteen miles north and south. All these kopjes were until the day of our attack occupied by a force of 7,000 Boers, but to the west of them were a few lower hills and ridges which we held. We did not know exactly how far to the east the Boer kopjes extended; that is to say, we did not know how broad might be the line of their defences; all we knew was that there were other kopjes to the eastward, and that the enemy probably held them. Our force, 30,000 strong, was disposed over a square of perhaps eight miles; yet if you had ridden all day in circles round the farm of Osfontein, which was Lord Roberts's headquarters, you might have wondered whether there were even 5,000 men, so scattered were our camps. The whole air of the place was that of almost pastoral quietness, and the only sound to be heard was the lowing of oxen.

Out in the advanced pickets the silence was deeper, but it was not pastoral. I rode out on the Monday to a little kopje, our most advanced post – a place within rifle range of the opposite Boer position, about 2,000 yards away. Over the plain, here green and sweet with the smell of tiny flowers newly burst out by the heavy rains, I rode out from under the shelter of a big kopje held by Kitchener's Horse. Between it and the little hill held by the picket the ground was exposed, but a man and a horse make a poor target at extreme range, and the danger was small.

We cantered along in the midst of the great harmonious silence of populous fields; the locusts waltzed in the sun, the little mere-cats stood and watched us for a moment and then scampered into their holes; the ants were toiling busily beneath a thousand heaps. The plain stretched to the horizon, with the stone-covered kopjes standing out like larger ant-heaps.

Something sang in the sunny air above my head, and I flicked with my whip to drive the locust away. Immediately afterwards I heard the sharp double report of a Mauser, like a postman's knock, and after that again the shrill moan, infinitely melancholy, of a flying bullet; and away to my left, about two hundred yards, the sand rose in a fountain. It was my first experience under fire, and I confess that for ten seconds I gave myself up. During those ten seconds I was altogether absorbed in watching a mere-cat trying to roll something into his house; then I began to see that I was not in any particular danger at so extreme a range, and I lost my interest in the mere-cat. But for all that my pony had to do his best over the space that separated us from the picket. There were a few more shots, and always the shrill moan, but in two minutes we were behind the shelter of the little hill.

I climbed up its steep side and found the handful of men, with an officer, lying among the stones on the windy height. There is no comfort in picket work. This officer and his men had to lie for twenty-four hours at a time without shelter from sun or rain, and with nothing to eat but bully beef and hard-tack biscuits. Always their glasses were sweeping the enemy's position, as the officer on a ship's bridge examines the horizon; every little movement of men or cattle was carefully noted.

Presently I had an illustration of the spirit in which lives are taken in war, a demonstration of what had been happening to myself a few minutes before. Out of the shoulder of a hill three Boers came on ponies, and began to walk leisurely across to the next kopje. Now immediately in front of our hill was another and smaller one, too inconsiderable to be occupied permanently, but useful for commanding the Boer front at rifle range. As we lay watching the three specks crossing the field, "Sergeant," said the officer, "take a few men down to that kopje, and see if you can't get a shot at the fellows." And off went the sergeant and a dozen men, as pleased as Punch.

Some time elapsed before they reached the hillock, and still the three Boers moved slowly and unsuspectingly across our view. After an anxious pause the rifles cracked out, one after another, like a rip-rap, and at the same time the Boers seemed to fly instead of to crawl. I then saw through my glasses that one of the men pitched backwards from his horse, which still fled, riderless now, beside the others, who were soon out of range. The men beside me cheered, but ten minutes ago I had been in a position exactly similar to that of the Boers; we are all egoists in such a case; it was myself that I saw out in the plain, my own pony rushing away scared; and I did not join in the acclamations. But all is changed in war-time; men are no more than game; the excitement is the old savage one – the lust of blood and the chase.

Late on the Tuesday night we heard that the attack was to be made early on the morrow. So we rose at three and rode out in the starlight through the busy camp, where the flashlights were talking and the fires blazing. I rode round to the south about eight miles, and presently the whole Boer position stood out black before the fires of dawn, and when the sun came up it showed one division of our troops – the Sixth – creeping round to the south where the enemy's position terminated in seven small kopjes. It was beautiful to see the division advance down the slope with the screen of mounted infantry opening out in front like a fan, with another and more slender screen, like another fan, in front of them again.

The sun was well up, but I had not yet heard a gun go off. Presently there was a report, and the sand rose in a column before the kopjes. This was a 4.7 naval gun finding its range with common shell. Again the invisible gun behind me boomed, again the weird, prolonged whirtling overhead; the long wait – perhaps for fifteen seconds; then a cloud of hideous vapour right on the kopje; then the report of the exploding shell. This happened perhaps half a dozen times; the well-aimed shells dropped now behind, now on the hills; there was no reply; and in half an hour the mounted infantry were riding over the kopjes. The enemy had simply broken and fled towards their central position.

From the north side, where the Ninth and Seventh Divisions were, one could hear the same sounds, but no rifle fire. After our guns had cleared the seven kopjes a kind of Sabbath stillness fell upon the land.

Lying in the grass, listening to the droning flies, I tried to tell myself that I was watching a momentous battle; that matters of life and death were on hand: but the wind laughed through the grasses at the very notion, and the timid steinbuck leaped up quite close to me, as if to say, "Who's afraid?"

Behind me a brigade was winding to the south with a movement almost lyrical; but no man seemed to be doing anything that could be called fighting. I decided that nothing more was to be seen on the south, and started to cross northward between the positions. My path was in what ought to have been the hottest zone of fire; but the hares leapt in the sun and the grasshoppers hummed with delight. While crossing northward I met the advance scouts of a regiment of mounted infantry advancing where, according to all ordinary laws, no mounted infantry could or ought to have been – advancing directly on the central Boer position.

"Come along," said the Colonel; "I believe the whole position is empty; we're going to scale those ridges."

Now these very ridges were the ones to which I had seen the Boers retreat, about a thousand of them, half an hour ago, and I told the Colonel so. "But they must have gone," he said, "or else they would be firing at us now."

It was perfectly true. The whole company was halted, while we chatted, within easy fire of the enemy's position; a few pom-poms would have made a shocking mess amongst the men and horses. But the hills were clothed with silence as with a garment.

"Anyhow, I'm going to see," said the Colonel. "Come along."

So we cantered on up to the foot of the hill, up the slope, over the hill, and not a shot was fired at us. The excitement was tremendous; we were riding slap into what looked like a hornets' nest. There were kopjes flanking us now on both sides; I wished that I hadn't come. I expected every moment to hear the rattle of Mausers. Someone's horse kicked a tin can, and we ducked our heads like one man. But we rode up to and into and through and over the central position of the enemy that he had been strengthening for days; and he never fired a shot to prevent us. It was glorious luck, thus to be in the very front of an advancing force, to be on the very horns of the advance, and to be absolutely out of danger, for what little opposition there was was encountered later by the main body.

When I thought that I had advanced far enough into what ought to have been the jaws of death, I drew on one side and let the brigade go past, and then I saw what little firing there was. Behind the mounted infantry came the field-guns, galloping alone over the smooth ground; and presently we heard the report of a gun from the other side of the next eastward ridge over which the enemy had retired. It is very uncomfortable waiting for a shell to arrive. One has only the sound to guide one as to where it has come from, and one has no notion at all as to where it is going to strike. This one burst right amongst the galloping artillery, which at once opened out on both sides of a smoking patch. Not a man or horse was down. And here the Boers lost their big chance of the day. All the brigade had to advance through this one narrow pass between the kopjes; the Boers had got the range of it absolutely; if they had fired a dozen shells in quick succession they would have done a dismal amount of mischief. But they only fired two other shells, and, marvellously, no one was hit. The reason I believe to have been that the dust of their own retreat, which hung like a haze over the ridge, hid our advancing troops from the Boers, and they did not know whether or not anyone was under their fire.

In the meantime the Ninth Brigade had been doing just the same kind of thing on the north river bank; and when the attack (such as it was – a gentle shelling) was being pressed there, General French came up from the south-east and drove the enemy northward across the river. If French had been a little earlier we should have cut off the Boers at the river, for that was their only line of retreat. As it was, he came in time to chase them; and when we heard of him again he was in full cry on the road to Bloemfontein.

It was a strange engagement; an almost bloodless battle; a great spectacle like an Aldershot Field Day; a demonstration of forces far stronger than the mere force of arms – confidence on the one hand, and on the other demoralisation and a broken spirit.

CHAPTER X

The March on Dreifontein

Early on the morning after the Osfontein engagement the army was again upon the march, and towards afternoon reached a farm called Poplar Grove, the point on which our left flank had rested on the day before. That was only a ten-mile journey, but men and beasts were tired, and a longer distance would have tried them severely. We rested a whole day at Poplar Grove, and many of us bathed in the river. It is strange indeed to find how comparative are all our standards of luxury; on that day you could have seen what Mr. Dooley might call the "flowers of the British aristocracy" splashing and rejoicing in filthy, muddy water beside Kaffirs and drinking mules; and no one who bathed on that day, after many days of wearing the same clothes and being impregnated with sand and sun, is likely to forget the luxury of the bath.

The discomforts of a hurried march are many, and the feeling of uncleanness is not the least of them; yet one recalls with pleasure the long days spent dozing along on one's horse at the head of a marching column that stretched seven miles over the plain and hills behind. Let me try to describe some of the circumstances of the march from Poplar Grove to Dreifontein. It must be remembered that these are but the names of farms, and that a farm means often nothing more than a mud house, a few trees, and a well of water.

Long before it was light we were awakened by the cries of Kaffirs collecting their ox teams and by the almost human complaints of many mules; and while we breakfasted by lamplight in the dim grove where our camp was pitched a stream of transport was already flowing out of the mass surrounding us on all sides. We started later, when the line along the east, crimson at first, had changed from saffron to bright gold, and the head of the column was already out of sight, melting towards the sunrise in a cloud of dust. The mounted infantry brigade, which furnished the patrols and screens, was already away scouring the plain in advance of the column, but the thin line of waggons was broken now by the broad shape of infantry brigades, marching fifty deep across the grass.

Our own small convoy was not got under weigh without many pains. The two newspapers which it represented were the proprietors of many and various beasts. Six riding ponies for the three correspondents, two horses for the despatch-rider, six horses to draw an American waggon and two Cape carts, and six oxen to draw an ox cart laden with forage. No tongue can tell the anxiety caused by those fourteen horses. No more could be bought, and if anything happened to them our usefulness would be at an end. I have often arisen during the night and walked down what we called our "lines," counting the beasts, and feeling like Abraham. To be sure, one of the horses cost but thirty shillings; we bought him from a Kaffir whose honesty I should be sorry to vouch for, but he could pull, and he lived more than a fortnight. For another one I paid a sovereign at Osfontein, but observing that he did not eat his supper one night I gently pushed him away a good hundred yards so that he should not die close to us.

By the time breakfast had been eaten, the oxen caught, the horses counted, the differences of six jealous servants adjusted, and the carts packed, we were ready to move off. Then the sun came up and the day began, and one could canter up to the front of the column, clear of the dust. On some days one rode up and down, visiting different regiments or finding out friends who were trudging beside their companies; but on the day of this march my pony was tired, and I let him amble along in front of the Guards for the whole eighteen miles.

I wish I could describe for people who have never seen it the grand and majestic march of 30,000 men with their guns and baggage across a large country; the slow dignity of a vast seven-mile column winding over the face of a plain, all the units diverging to pass the same ant-heap or to avoid the same rough place. After the first few miles it is silent, and one hears behind one only the sweep of many feet upon the grass. It is like Fate, or, say, Time with his scythe held steady; the thing comes and passes and is gone; but ride backward and you shall see the traces of its passage. Grass downtrodden that shall rise again, little flowers bruised that shall renew their blossoms; and still the birds singing peacefully, the hares leaping, the manifold petty life of the veldt resuming its routine and circumstance. One passes on through the quaking air as in a dream, and as though impelled by the great force behind; and to eyes gazing long on the ground the affairs of tiny creatures become conspicuous and important. The mere-cats sit listening, and wonder what the new sound in the grass means, not like wind or rain. Little lizards basking on the sand suddenly wake up and wriggle away to avoid the thing against which the shelter of a leaf will not avail them. And always in front hares and buck by the hundred stream away like the shadows of clouds over grass. Then someone looks at his watch and shouts "Halt!" and the welcome word is shouted and repeated down the line until the sound is lost in the distance, while the tired men throw themselves down between the burning sun and the sand.

It is like sailing on a wide sea after a storm, when the short and high waves have died away beneath the tread of smooth rollers. The veldt undulates from sky to sky, a plain rising and falling about the base of rocks and island kopjes. One reaches the crest, hoping for a new view, searching for the clump of trees that means a farm and fresh water; and one sinks down again into the furrow, while the wave of disappointment runs backward along the seven miles of column as each man rises to the barren view. Now an ox, now a mule or a horse falls out and lies down to die; now a man stumbles and falls, and lies down to wait for the cool hours.

To men who find this kind of monotony irksome the march is a dreary business, while to others its bare outline is filled with the interest of a thousand little happenings. The tired, dusty, shabby "Tommy" is a man much more agreeable to talk with than his ancestor of the barrack-room at home; the youngest subaltern has forgotten all about his swagger mess-kit and the "style" of his regiment, and shows himself as the good fellow he is; even the Brigadier forgets the scarlet on his khaki collar, and remembers that he too is a frail mortal. And always, when other interest failed, one could fall back on that of one's own sometimes troublesome affairs. On the afternoon of the Dreifontein march our advance cart with the luncheon had not outspanned fifteen minutes before it was discovered that one of the horses was gone. There was no doubt as to why, of course – a soldier had "snaffled" it. I am sorry to say that in the matter of horse property the average Tommy holds vague moral views. That cart had to be brought into camp by night, and there was only one way in which it could be done. I rode about for ten minutes, and found an old framework so thin and so dejected that I blushed when I put the halter on it; it had been abandoned on account of lameness, from which it had recovered, and had since been starving. They harnessed it up and it brought in the cart; and that night, being given a good feed of oats, it died from shock. Another skeleton was found in the morning to take its place; but this skeleton grew fat. We used to laugh at these misfortunes, but the poor horses had a cruel time, especially the English ones; no one would have recognised the Horse Artillery, although the tragic skeletons that drew the guns still affected some imitation of their old dash. All the way from Modder to Bloemfontein was strewn with the bodies of horses; if all other marks had been gone, these melancholy quarter-mile posts would have guided you unerringly.

It was night as a rule before the column reached its camp, and there were some gorgeous pictures in the great outspanning commotion seen through dust clouds and the red sunset, and by light of many camp fires. But on this bit of the march we found our quarters sooner than we expected; and it was early in the afternoon when, climbing the ridge of undulating plain, I saw the smoke of a shell bursting on the hillside five miles away, and knew that our day's march, though not our day's work, was at an end.

CHAPTER XI

The Battle of Dreifontein and the March On Bloemfontein

A great chain of kopjes barred the horizon ahead of us, and we came to the usual conclusion that the Boers were opposing our advance. It is well to remember that Lord Roberts's army was not marching in a single column, but in three separate columns, of which the Cavalry Division was marching on a road about six miles to the north, and the Seventh Division by a road about four miles to the south of the main body. General French was a day's march ahead of the main army, and on this morning he reached Abraham's Kraal (the most northerly hill of the chain held by the Boers) at ten o'clock, while the Ninth Division did not arrive until four o'clock. It will thus be seen that one end of the position was a couple of hours' ride distant from the other and far out of sight of it.

No one saw the whole of the battle of Dreifontein. General French, when he arrived at ten in the morning, came into contact with the Boers at Abraham's Kraal, and (the river preventing a turning movement on the north) he sent the second cavalry brigade galloping southward down the line of the kopjes in order to turn, if possible, the enemy's left flank. But he soon found that the position extended too far southward to be assailable by his limited forces. This turning movement, or rather the preparation for it, was carried out under an extremely heavy fire from pom-poms and other quick-firing guns. Finding that his resources would be exhausted in drawing out the long containing thread necessary to hold the enemy in front, and so leave nothing with which to make a flank attack, General French contented himself with engaging the enemy on the northernmost end of their position.

At half-past one the Sixth Division arrived at Dreifontein, a farmhouse about seven miles south of Abraham's Kraal. I had ridden hard in order to catch them up as I had been in the early morning with the Ninth Division, which did not arrive until four o'clock, and when I came up I was just in time to see the Buffs, leading the 13th Brigade, preparing to clear some kopjes near the main ridge which were held by the Boers. Things were very hot here, and as I had never been in a big fight before I found it very difficult to realise what was going on, or where the enemy was, or where the fire was coming from, or at what point it was being directed. All I knew for some time was that there were shells dropping rather closer than was pleasant, and that with a rashness born of ignorance I had got into a place where everyone had to lie down for cover.

When your face is in the sand you do not see much. What you hear is not encouraging – the distant boom of a gun, a few seconds' silence, then a long quavering whistle in the air, like the cry of a banshee, growing every moment nearer and louder, and finally the deafening report somewhere near you. You never know where a shell is going to burst, although you hear it long before it arrives; you can only sit tight and hope that it will go where the other fellows are, or better still where no one is. To say truth, shells generally go where no one is; I saw only one man killed by a shell. I had raised my head from the ground and was listening for the burst of a coming shell, when I saw a man among the advance ranks of the 13th Brigade on my right stop suddenly in the midst of a blinding flash. An arm and hand flew through the air in a horrible curve; the smoke belched, the air was rent by the explosion, the smoke blew and drifted away, and there on the hillside lay what was left of the man, folded in the deep quietness of death.

A little to the left the Welsh Regiment was advancing up the steep side of Alexander's kopje, which was doubly enfiladed by the Boer guns; two Elswicks firing from the east and a Vickers-Maxim from the south-west. There was also a nasty rain of bullets. In the long semi-circular skirmishing line, strung like a girdle round the hillside, a man suddenly turned and ran backwards for half a dozen paces, and then tumbled, rolling over and over like a shot rabbit. I saw him five minutes later when his body was brought to the dressing-station; he had been shot through the heart. Poor fellow! He ran not of his own conscious volition; he was killed while bravely advancing; he died while retreating. The Welsh Regiment was losing badly all this time, and the ground was becoming dotted with writhing and motionless bodies; it was a horrible sight and came near to turning me sick, so I resolved to go and see what was happening on the south side.

I made a long detour round by the headquarter farmhouse towards which the black mass of the Ninth Division was advancing across the plain – too late, as it turned out, to join in the action. Seeing a kopje on our extreme right from which our artillery seemed to be firing, I rode in that direction. There was not a soul in sight; and when I was within a thousand yards of the place the instinct which so often interferes to keep our heads from betraying us made me pull up. There was not a sound except the far-away bang of guns and rifles. Near to the kopje there was a garden surrounded by low trees and a hedge of prickly pear.

The sun setting behind us slanted into it and made it appear as a charming, peaceful shelter from the dust and noise of the battle. I was still debating with myself as to whether I should go on a little farther when I heard behind me the sound of a horse galloping. I turned round and saw, perhaps two miles behind me, three mounted men. The one who now rode up had evidently just left them. He was a trooper in Rimington's Guides.

"Beg pardon, sir," he said, "but I wouldn't stay here if I was you."

"Why not?" said the Green One; "no one in front, is there?"

The man spat on the ground.

"Don't know that there is, sir," he said, "but then I don't know that there isn't, and that's good enough for me. If there *is* anyone in that garden" – and he pointed to the patch of trees – "you bet they won't send out a flag of truce asking you to get out of the way before they shoot. We've been sent to round up cattle out of that there garden, but I believe the cattle are all a blind. Anyway, I'm not going near it till I'm sure of it. I believe it's a trap."

They must have been watching us from the garden with their eyes on the sights of their rifles, for no sooner had we turned our horses' heads than *bang, bang, bang, bang – phtt, phtt, phtt, phtt!* We doubled ourselves on our saddles and our horses stretched along the road, while for perhaps thirty seconds our ears twitched to a hail of bullets that lasted until we were out of range. While we were still racing my pony, which was last, suddenly jumped into the air and shot past the big cavalry horse, laying herself flat on the ground like a hare; and it was not until she had carried me far out of range that I found the warm blood from a bullet wound running down her leg. I had no further interest that day but to have her attended to. At any rate, I think the shot which was fired at her was one of the last fired in the battle of Dreifontein.

The battle was fought on Saturday, March 10th. On Sunday morning we found that the Boers had melted away from before us, and the army marched on twelve miles to Aasvögel's Kop. On Monday the main body was at Venters Vlei; and at four o'clock that afternoon General French, after an artillery engagement, occupied a few hills commanding Bloemfontein, and sent in an ultimatum requiring the surrender of the town within twenty-four hours.

Early on Tuesday morning Mr. Gwynne (Reuter's correspondent), Mr. Oppenheim, of the *Daily News*, and another correspondent, rode into Bloemfontein and found that President Steyn had departed during the night, that the Boer forces had retired from the immediate neighbourhood of the town, and that the people were willing to surrender. They rode back to Lord Roberts (who was by this time well under weigh with his column), escorting the Landdrost in his Cape cart. The Field Marshal was, I believe, sitting on a low hill having breakfast with his staff when the keys were delivered up to him. This formality was conducted with the utmost courtesy and good-humour, and when it was over the march was resumed. Lord Roberts rode on and joined the cavalry, and a procession was formed about three miles out of the town, Lord Roberts at the head of the cavalry brigade which preceded the army. I shall never forget that ride down the sloping country into Bloemfontein; the little white-haired man sitting his horse like a rock, leading; then the personal staff; then the general staff; then the foreign attachés; then the correspondents; then the cavalry staff; then the cavalry; then the main body of the army – artillery, infantry, engineers, commissariat, and baggage.

As we came into the first street of the town it was apparent that the day was regarded as a festival. One could hardly imagine a stranger reception of an invader. Flags flew at every window, and the people were all decked out as though for a holiday. Half-way towards the Presidency there was a little diversion. Some Kaffirs, thinking that this was a good opportunity of paying off old scores, had begun to loot and pillage a large building like a school-house, which belonged to the Free State Government. As we swung round the corner of the street they were in the act of bundling out mattresses, bedsteads, linen, chairs, desks, and tables, and carrying them off. A few dozen Lancers were let loose amongst them; they dropped their booty and fled, only to be driven back at the point of a lance and made to replace the stolen property. Then the march was resumed until the procession drew up in front of the Presidency. The Federal flag had been struck some time before, and the flagstaff now stood gaunt and undecorated. There was a pause of about ten minutes while Lord Roberts went in and transacted some necessary formalities; then the little silk Union Jack, made by Lady Roberts, was run up to the truck amid a great sound of cheering. The singing of the National Anthem ended the ceremony. The town seemed altogether English – English shops, English manners, the English language, and English faces. All that day enthusiasm bubbled in the town like water boiling in a pot; all day the troops continued to march in; shabby and dusty and dirty and tired, they were nevertheless all stamped with some nameless quality which they had not when they left England. All day the population of Bloemfontein eddied through the streets like a crowd at a fair; all day the sounds of rejoicing continued, and far into the night the streets resounded to the cries of people who made merry.

CHAPTER XII

Retracing the Steps of the Army

With its independence, handed over amid the imposing circumstance of arms, Bloemfontein lost something of its charm. The noise and dust and commotion of the army did violence to its pastoral quietness, and the pretty shops put up their shutters at midday as though in maidenly horror at the eagerness of crowds of soldiers running amuck like children with their Saturday pennies. I entered the town early enough to see what its normal condition must be, and there was something rude and unkind in the din of the multitude breaking on this quiet place where the bees sang loud in the streets, and the midday idler slumbered upon the doorstep.

To be sure, one had opportunity for studying the soldier in a new setting, but the study is one that requires time; the average Tommy is an oyster to strangers. He varies to the tune and colour of his surroundings; on the veldt, where hardness is to be endured, he is the "good soldier," the patient, strong man; under fire he is a fierce creature, still obedient to his habit of discipline, but hot for combat; in the town, with money in his pocket, he is a little child. Indeed, after weeks of absence from places where money is of value we all share in this rejuvenation, and if you had been in Bloemfontein on any one of these fine days you would have seen men of every age and rank, from generals to trumpeters, wandering about the streets, agape at the shop windows, chinking their money in their pockets, and buying things for which they had no kind of use.

The British officer afield is a very different creature from the gilded ornament of an English mess. His face is scorched and peeled, he is generally (unless he be a staff officer) very ill-clad; he has a ragged beard; he esteems golden syrup the greatest luxury on earth; he ceases to be ashamed of originality in thought or expression; he altogether fails to disguise what a good fellow he is. But in a very short time the neighbourhood of a club, the possibility of a bath, the presence of barbers and tailors, by a mysterious and marvellous working, reverse his development, and the little graces which endear him to society at home begin to reappear. So long as the sole of his boot was tied to the uppers by a piece of string, he could not look you in the face with any pretending; but when the cobbler has done his office, and the tailor has sewn up the rent breeches, the spell is broken.

60

We "occupied" Bloemfontein so completely that, after the first few days, I was glad to take the road again. We occupied the club, we occupied the shops and hotels, we occupied even the homes of the simple townspeople; and we occupied the streets, so that all day the town resounded to the din of tramping feet. When one has slept for a month under the stars, sheets and a roof are stifling; so as the railway was not yet open, Major Pollock (of *The Times*) and I decided to go to Kimberley by road, assured that the moral effect of the proclamation would keep us out of danger from the Queen's enemies.

Our little caravan set forth by moonlight, taking the road travelled by the left-hand column of the three parallel columns that had advanced on Bloemfontein, and somewhat to the north of that taken by Lord Roberts and the central column, with which we had gone in. The journey itself was uneventful enough, full of the little interests and anxieties and pleasures of the road, full of joy for the travellers, but without serious interest to anyone else. There was just enough risk of encountering a commando to give the necessary spice of adventure; two despatch-riders – not mine, by the good fortune of half a mile – had been captured the day before, and we kept a bright look-out. But by the time we came across them the commandos were forlornly[2]dispersing. For the rest, there was the unending charm of the climate and the place; the gorgeous evenings, when sunset and moonrise encircled the horizon in a flame of gold and silver; the spring-cold mornings, with the veldt glowing from violet to purple and crimson; the noonday rest in some deserted farm garden; the bed at nightfall, with the sound of horses munching their corn for a lullaby – all the circumstances of simple travel accomplished by the means that nature has provided. After having been for so long in the company of 30,000 men we found the loneliness and quietness refreshing, and we passed almost unnoticed through the birds and beasts and flowers. We swam once more in the muddy Modder, now quite an old friend. The track of the army was marked for us in two ways – one ludicrous, the other tragic; both unmistakable. For all along the way bright tin biscuit canisters of the Army Service Corps shone like diamonds in the sun; and all along the way, at intervals, tired and sick old cavalry horses stood by the roadside, each surrounded by a crowd of foul aasvögels, the vultures of South Africa, waiting.

The chief party of Boers which we encountered was at Abraham's Kraal. While we were breakfasting about two dozen of them cantered up, of whom about six were armed. If I had qualms, I hope I did not show them when I said "Good-morning." I fell into conversation with one of

---

[2] For the time being.

the Boers, and mentioned incidentally that, from their point of view, the game was up, and that I supposed he knew that anyone who interfered with peaceful Englishmen would be hanged. He was a sulky fellow, but he took my word for it, and presently we began to talk. These Boers were in low spirits about the war, and spoke of it without enthusiasm or hope. Most of them were Transvaalers, and two spoke with an unmistakable Glasgow accent, but on the whole they were gruff and uncommunicative, and, as they cast envious eyes from their own sorry nags to our well-conditioned mounts, I was glad to wish them good-day. They had come to bury the dead from the Dreifontein fight, and from what they told me of the still unburied Boers both there and at Paardeberg, I gathered that their casualties all along the line had been heavier than we had thought.

I have said that the neighbourhood of the Boers made our journey exciting, and there was one point at which the excitement became very nearly painful. We had made a long stage one day, and at about sundown arrived at the Modder, which we intended to cross at a drift near Koodoesrand. This was the dangerous neighbourhood, and we were anxious to push on and cross the river before encamping for the night. The banks of the Modder at this drift are about forty feet high and almost precipitous, the path down to the drift being little better than a track worn at a long diagonal down the bank. It was steep enough going down, but when we had crossed the shallow river and begun the ascent of the other bank we found the track very soft and almost perpendicular. By fetching a compass and putting the horses to it at a great pace the two Cape carts managed to reach the top, but a four-wheeled American waggon stuck fast at the bottom and could not be moved. At that moment the last of the daylight ebbed, and darkness began to quench the sunset embers.

We tried unhitching the teams from the Cape carts and hitching them to the waggon, but we only succeeded in breaking harness. It was after the second attempt, when we were all standing hot and angry after our unavailing exertion of whip-cracking and shouting, that we suddenly saw a light shine out from the edge of a low kopje about two miles in front of us. One of us lost his head, and by speaking his fears communicated the malady.

"There are the Boers," he said, "and if they haven't heard us yelling they must have seen the light from our lanterns. The sooner we get out of this the better."

There was nothing for it but to unload the waggon and carry the contents up by hand, and this we did in an agony of excitement, staggering and sweating up the steep path with portmanteaus, beds, valises, cases of tinned provisions, kettles, bottles, saucepans, bags of harness, oats, and guns. The empty waggon was easily drawn up to the top, and then we must reload it again with a burden which seemed to have swollen enormously since it was unpacked. We were working so frantically that we had not even time to look at the kopje, but when at length I glanced at it I saw that a strange thing had happened.

The light was now suspended about thirty feet above the hill.

Had they a balloon? Major Pollock and I gazed blankly for more than a minute at that mysterious shining, which seemed to rise higher and higher. More than a minute: just so long did it take us to remember that Orion rises low in the west!

Now for what will remain with me as the crowning impression of this journey. The road we took led through a fairly fertile country, and that in the Free State means that there generally was grass instead of karoo. There were many farms; we probably passed twenty in the course of ninety miles. Each of those farms I visited, and at each stood aghast at the ruin that had been wrought. Signs of looting one expected – the looting of food-stuffs and livestock and necessaries; that, after all, is but a kind of self-defence, and I suppose it is allowable to live upon an enemy when one invades his land. But the destruction that had here taken place was wanton and savage. One seemed to travel in the footsteps of some fiend who had left his mark upon every home, destroying the things that were probably most prized by the owners, and destroying with a devilish ingenuity that had saved him all unnecessary labour. For example, in one little farmhouse I found a flimsy, showy, London bedroom suite that was clearly the pride of the establishment, with its wardrobe and full-length mirror. The destroyer had smashed just what could not be mended – the mirror and the marble top of the washstand. In another cottage I found an old clock that had ticked, most likely, for years on end in the quietness of the little home; its hands were torn off, and its works strewn upon the floor. In every house the little bits of rubbish that adorn the homes of the poor were destroyed or disfigured; in all were the same signs of violation, the same marks of the beast.

It has always seemed to me that a little farm in a lonely country contains more than anything else the atmosphere of a home. It is self-centred; there you see all the little shifts and contrivances which result from the forced supplying of wants that cannot be satisfied from outside. And when such a homestead is deserted, I think the atmosphere is only the more pronounced; the disused implements find voices in the silence and cry aloud for their absent owners. But when all that is personal and human in such a place is ruined, the pathos turns to tragedy. One farm I found absolutely gutted save for a great and old Bible which stood upon a table in the largest room. It was a beautiful folio, full of quaint plates and fine old printing, and bound in a rich leather that time and the sun had tanned to an autumn gold. While I was regarding it the breeze came through the window and stirred the yellow leaves, exposing a pencil-marked verse in the most pastoral of psalms: "*Hy doert my nederliggen in grasige wenden; Hy doert my sachtkens aen seer stille wateren.*" There was something impressive in the accident: the old book stoutly reminding the chance passer-by that present evil cannot affect the ultimate good, promising amid rude circumstances a time of quietness. He was an old man who owned that book; his name and age were marked upon the leaf; I think, to judge by the signs of handling, that he had the heart of its contents; and I hope that whatever his bodily circumstances, his soul retained some of the peace of the "*grasige wenden.*"

Who is responsible for all this mischief it is hard to say. I am sure that the English soldiers, thoughtless though they may be, would not stoop to this sort of purposeless outrage. I do not like to accuse the colonial troops as a whole either, although I suspect that some of them, some whose own homes had been destroyed by the enemy, might conceivably have taken vengeance in kind. It is thought by many whose opinion is valuable that the Kaffirs were here, as in Natal, responsible for much of the damage; and that is a view which one would willingly take, for it would acquit English-speaking troops of a miserable suspicion. Perhaps the thing is well-nigh inevitable, for I know what pains Lord Roberts took to prevent it; and it may be as well that we should recognise it as one of the realities of war. For myself, the horrors of actual fighting did not touch me half so nearly; I have seen men killed close to me and been less shocked than I was by these domestic outrages. To die, for the one who dies, is nothing; it affects him not at all; he is absent. But here was not death, but outrage on the foundations of civilised life; outrage upon living people, who suffer and remember.

PART IV

An Expedition With Lord Methuen

CHAPTER XIII

In the Field Again

After all, we need not have made so much haste to leave Bloemfontein. We had been told there that a column would start for the relief of Mafeking on March 20th, but when we arrived at Kimberley on the 18th we found that no movement was to take place for several days. The date was constantly shifted farther into the future, and the days of waiting had grown into weeks before an order came that Lord Methuen with his force of about 10,000 men was to march on Boshof. As far as information went we lived from hand to mouth; all the orders came from Bloemfontein, and they seldom provided for more than a day at a time. It was not unnatural, therefore, that when an order to move did at last come we built upon it all kinds of extravagant expectations, and it was a cheerful army that left Kimberley on April 2nd and took the road for Boshof.

After many days of inaction it was indeed good to recommence a moving life among oxen and waggons and guns and soldiers. Kimberley was all very well as a spectacle immediately after the siege; everyone flocked to see the holes in the houses and the ruined buildings. It was all very well (so, at any rate, we persuaded ourselves) to live in a club and to dine again amid damask and flowers and cut glass after the rude life of the fields; but even this was a novelty only for a day, and one soon became impatient of the poor shift at living which dwellers in towns are forced to make. I think I never saw a town so lost and drowned beneath the wave of money-getting as Kimberley; even its recent privations were turned to a nimble account, and 6-inch shells were selling at £10 apiece before I left. The people who fled most readily from the projectiles were of course the most eager to buy them – so highly do we esteem the instruments which make us seem heroes to ourselves. For the moment Kimberley transferred its attentions commercially from diamonds to shells: a less romantic and (if you will believe it) a more sordid industry; for there were already more storied and pedigreed shells in private collections and for sale in Kimberley than ever fell into the town.

Boshof, at any rate, provided a welcome change from all this. It is a pretty little town of greensward streets and clear brooks; of white cottages embowered in trees; of rose-gardens and orchards; rather like a remote country town in Ireland – poor and pretty and sleepy. There were few able-bodied men left in it, and aged people looked doubtfully out from their fuchsia-covered doors upon the ranks and regiments of foreign soldiers who came clattering through the streets on some of those hot April afternoons. We were to advance, it was now thought, on the 6th; in what direction we did not know certainly, but we suspected that it would be along the Hoopstad Road. The arguments and speculations with which we occupied ourselves need not be recorded now, but it was at once our hope and fear that we should advance along the north bank of the Vaal. Hope, because there was work to be done there; fear, lest our smaller force should be absorbed by Lord Roberts's larger army and become merely its left flank. Events showed that we might have spared ourselves both hopes and fears, but fortunately we were ignorant, and so found occupation for many an hour that had otherwise been empty.

An interval of inaction in the midst of a war is tedious in some ways, but it is at least of benefit to a mere onlooker, who is thus enabled to disengage himself from the whirl of operations and to discover the results of his unwonted occupation. After having lived amongst soldiers – in some ways and in spite of their profession the most human and civilised of men – it had come upon me as a shock to find in Kimberley the same bloodthirstiness that had distinguished the more thoughtless section of the public at home. Cruel shouting for blood by people who never see it; the iteration of that most illogical demand, a life for a life – and, if possible, two lives for a life; the loud, hectoring, frothy argument that lashes itself into a fury with strong and abusive language – they all came like a clap of thunder after what I am bound to call in comparison the quiet decency of the battlefield. This is a grave thing to say, but it would be unfair to disguise so clear an impression as this that I received, who went to South Africa with so little political bias that eager partisans of neither colour in Cape Town would own me. To appear lukewarm amongst people who are red-hot is not always pleasant, but it has its compensations; one has at least a foothold – inglorious, perhaps, but safe and desirable in a dizzy world.

It was impossible to be in Kimberley and not to become involved in the endless political discussions of clubs and dinner tables. I used to try very hard to discover what it was that made the average Briton living in South Africa hate the Boers so bitterly. The Colonial despises the Boer, but one does not hate a man only because one despises him. Jealousy is the best blend with contempt, and there is no doubt that the Boer's not unnatural desire to be paramount in his own land was what English colonists with whom I talked chiefly resented. We might talk for an hour or for a day – the same old grievances always came round: the inferior political position of the Uitlanders, the primitive, not to say dirty and slovenly, habits of many Boer farmers, and their lack of energy. These are the grievances of the man in the street, and they appear grave enough – when once one has invested oneself with the right of censorship. Then the rebels – wretched, unsuccessful farmers, who found themselves misled and their ideas of duty confounded – these were the chief objects of the lust for revenge. A rebel, as a man who has tried unsuccessfully to overthrow by force the Government to which he owes allegiance, must expect to suffer; but even in the case of these miserable creatures there is surely a scale of responsibility to be observed and a measure of justice to be meted. If Kimberley or Cape Town had ruled the matter by their mass meetings nearly every rebel would have been hanged – a very poor way, one would think, of making loyal subjects. But the reasons that were urged in support of such drastic punishment were astonishingly frank: "It doesn't pay to be loyal," one was told; "we might as well have been rebels." Not a very lofty form of patriotism.

One came to shrink from using that grand word, so plausible a cloak did it become for much that is mean and degrading. For example, when I was riding from Bloemfontein to Kimberley I and my companion descried a farmhouse two miles in front of us near Koodoesrand Drift; when we had come within about a mile of it a little travesty of a Union Jack was run up on a stick, and when we rode up to the door a farmer came out, smiling, rubbing his hands, sniggering – in a word, truckling. His talk was like the political swagger of the music-hall or the butler's pantry.

"I'm John Bull to the core – eh? No damned Boers for me – eh? Ha, ha, wipe 'em out, gentlemen, wipe 'em out: old England's all right as long as we've got gentlemen like you to defend us – eh?" (He took us for officers.) "John Bull for ever – eh?"

And while he spoke someone inside the house played "God Save the Queen" with one finger (incorrectly) on a harmonium. The incident had a more unpleasant flavour than I can well convey; we went away feeling ashamed.

All this belongs to the dark side of the campaign; fortunately there was another, how bright I cannot say, that went far to make one forget the rest. For the soldier the whole moral question had been decided; his duty was so clear that he never needed to hesitate. And his blood would have been sluggish indeed who must not have been stirred to the heart by these inspiring circumstances: whether in camp, where the population of a town was housed and fed in an hour, every man charged with some duty for the common benefit, the whole a pattern of social administration; or on the march, with the scouts and patrols opening and spreading in advance and covering every patch of ground for miles round, the sweep and imposing measure of the marching troops, the miles of supply and baggage waggons, each in its appointed place; or on the battlefield, where troops were handled and man[oe]uvred as on a chessboard, where men went to death with light hearts, lying for perhaps hours under fire, stealing a piece of ground here or a bit of cover there, with one eye on their officer and another on the flash before them, and perhaps a thought in the middle of it all for someone at home – there, indeed, where stern duties were faithfully fulfilled was set a great example. Fortunately for some of us at home the men who direct and conduct our battles are magnanimous, and one had the gratification of seeing, even upon occasions so savage, little acts of courtesy and humanity rendered on both sides that went far to take the sting out of a defeat.

And let there be no mistake about the Boers as soldiers. In spite of the far too numerous abuses of the rules of civilised warfare by detached and independent combatants – abuses, it should be remembered, that have occurred and will occur in every war and in the ranks of every army – our officers and men have a genuine respect and admiration for their enemy. No one looked upon death at their hands as anything but honourable. And as one's admiration and sympathy were stirred for one's own fellow-countrymen, who so unflinchingly performed their duties, could one withhold it from that other army five miles away across the plain – citizen soldiers fighting for their country and their homes? For the soldier politics do not exist; he fights and dies for an idea. This is mere sentiment, you may say, instead of fact about arms and battles; yet the hardest fact that rings beneath your stamp is no more real than poor, flimsy sentiment, which is a living force in the world, and will remain to be reckoned with when pom-poms and Creusots are rusting in archæological museums – monuments only to the mechanical and political clumsiness of the nineteenth century.

CHAPTER XIV

The Capture of Boers at Tweefontein

Lord Methuen had not long to wait for occupation. As soon as he arrived at Boshof he posted his pickets on every possible point of vantage, and patrolled the neighbourhood of Boshof over a wide circumference; and he was rewarded. The little engagement at Tweefontein was, we all hoped, an auspicious beginning for Lord Methuen's advance. If one might apply the word to military tactics, it was as artistic a piece of work as could be. I do not remember a single mistake or an instance of anything less well or less quickly done than was possible. The result was a raising of everyone's spirits, and I thought that Lord Methuen himself had the air of a man emerging from depression. Certainly no general was better liked by those around him, and, in spite of all mischievous gossip to the contrary, he was perfectly trusted by his officers and men.

On Friday morning, April 6th, a native guide came in with information that the enemy had a laager at a farm called Tweefontein, nine miles south-east of Boshof. In ten minutes Major Streatfeild had his horse packed and saddled and was off to the Yeomanry camp. Now the Yeomanry horses were out on the plain grazing a good mile away; yet from the time when the order was given until the moment of starting exactly thirty-five minutes elapsed – a performance that would not have disgraced veterans. The artillery and the Kimberley Mounted Corps (an excellent force, although not so well horsed as the Yeomanry) were ready in the same time, and the force started in the following order: Scouts of the Kimberley Mounted Corps; advance guard ditto; Staff; Imperial Yeomanry, under Lord Chesham; Fourth Company Royal Artillery; Kimberley Mounted Corps, under Lieut.-Colonel Peakman.

When the force was within three miles of Tweefontein the scouts returned, stating that the only kopje in the neighbourhood was held by the enemy. The native guides had led us by an excellent road and with absolute accuracy, and the enemy had no idea of our presence until we came up over the ridge and showed our force in the centre. Lord Methuen then developed his attack, which, as the kopje was isolated, was on the simple plan of a centre with two extending wings. There was a delay in the centre until Captain Rolleston's (Lieutenant-Colonel commanding Nottinghamshire Yeomanry) company, under Lord

Scarborough, could get into position on the left. The enemy opened fire without delay, so the Yeomanry had to make a wide detour. Meanwhile the centre was held back while the Kimberley Mounted Corps, under Colonel Peakman, were sent to the right, where they found cover in a ridge of very low kopjes.

When both flanks were in position the main body of Yeomanry dismounted and advanced towards the kopje in extended order. Now was their time. You must remember that this was their baptism of fire, and everyone was on the look-out for signs of "greenness"; everyone had more or less been making fun of them in a mild way, and prophesying all sorts of disaster. As they advanced the bullets began to pipe on the edge of the firing-zone, but there was not a bit of change in the Yeomanry when they came under fire. I know from experience how disconcerting it is to ride into the zone of fire, and walking must be much worse. It is not half so bad when you are fairly in; it is like wading into a cold and shallow sea instead of plunging – a kind of shivering sensation, most unpleasant. Well, they went through this nasty belt as coolly as you please – no hurry or funk. They dropped like wax when the order came to lie down, and fired steadily.

The whole of our little field was now under fire, and the cavalry on each side were keeping the Boers very busy. All the time the right and left flanks were opening out and reaching towards each other behind the kopje. The only disappointment was that the artillery could not get to work; the rise of the ground was so great and we had covered the position so completely that it was rather dangerous to attempt shelling. For about two hours there was hot firing, and every now and then there was a little work for our ambulance people, but not much. The only noticeable evidence of inexperience on the part of the Yeomanry was that they did not realise – and no one can realise this when fighting the Boers for the first time – how great is the enemy's firing range, and how far away one must keep to be able to live at all. They kept pressing forward, and Major Streatfeild had to ride across from the General under a very hot fire to tell them to keep back.

Towards the end of the engagement there was a gap in front of the artillery position, and the guns spoke. They got the range at once, and fired three rounds of shrapnel, and a few minutes after the third round had been fired a white flag was waved from the hill. Silence fell like a shadow over the place that had been crackling with fire a minute before; people who had been lying flat on the ground stood up and stretched themselves; and in the midst of the silence a shot cracked from the hill, and there was a rush of men towards a prostrate body on our side. Then another shot cracked – from our side this time; the treacherous Boer, I was told, fell dead, and the action was over.

We captured fifty-two prisoners, and the Boers had eight killed and six wounded. No one escaped. They all laid down their arms and surrendered, handing over also a cart of dynamite. From this it was gathered that General Villebois (who was killed) had been trying to get behind us to the railway line near Modder River, where he hoped to destroy it. I spoke to some of the prisoners next day – Frenchmen, many of them, and nice enough fellows. I heard then something which gave me pause with regard to the white flag. When the thing happened it appeared to be a flagrant and indubitable case of treachery; everyone was speaking of it. But one of the prisoners, in talking to me, referred to the "rascal" who showed the flag.

"We had no intention to surrender," he said; "no order was given; that worm had a flag in his pocket, and he held it up; poor----(mentioning the man who shot and was killed) probably never saw it. It's a wonder half of us did not go on firing."

I give this statement for what it is worth. "All lies" was the comment of some of the officers there, and quite possibly they were right; but quite possibly also they were wrong, and the whole thing was an accident. At least one may learn a lesson from it. I hated to believe it, but I believed it to be treachery. Now it turns out that I may have been unjust, and possibly on a dozen other occasions the same sort of involuntary injustice may have been done to our enemies. Certainly it is much easier for soldiers to see a small conspicuous object when it is displayed by the enemy than when it is displayed by one of their own side. The men on either side are intent upon watching the other side, not their own.

In General Villebois de Mareuil's pocket was found a note-book containing a cleverly planned diagram of an attack on Boshof, and when the sun was setting he was buried in the town he had hoped to enter victoriously. It was a most impressive ceremony; the slanting sun, the imposing military honours, the solemn words of the office – it is easily imagined; it will not be easily forgotten by those of us who witnessed it. Next morning we had left Boshof and its green streets behind, and were winding along the road, the line of patrols sweeping like a long billow over the hills before and on each side of us. We paused for a night at Zwaartzkopjesfontein, went on the next morning to Mahemsfontein; whence, having received orders from Lord Roberts to halt, we fell back on Zwaartzkopjesfontein.

On Monday morning, April 9th, I went out with the Yeomanry, who made a reconnaissance ten miles to the east. We found a party of about sixty Boers chasing goats and cattle and stock of all kinds on a Dutch farm occupied only by women. We could see them through glasses driving the stock away (about sixty head), but they only fired a shot or two at one of our scouts, and then fled, taking and keeping a four-mile start of us. This expedition was at least interesting, as again showing the really excellent work and methods of the Yeomanry. They cared for their horses in a more intelligent way than any regular cavalry I have seen, and they were not above taking hints from the Colonials in the matter of marching and patrolling order. Everyone was surprised. It had been quite the thing to smile at the very mention of the Yeomanry; yet they speedily proved themselves quite equal to take their place beside any other of the Volunteers, even the best of the Colonial mounted corps.

With a charming courtesy Lord Methuen designed and erected at his own expense a monument over the grave of his fallen enemy. On the stone is engraved this inscription: –

A LA MEMOIRE
DU COMTE DE VILLEBOIS DE MAREUIL
ANCIEN COLONEL
DE LA LEGION ÉTRANGÈRE
EN FRANCE
GÉNÉRAL DU TRANSVAAL
MORT AU CHAMP D'HONNEUR
PRÈS DE BOSHOF
LE 5 AVRIL, 1900
DANS SA 53ème ANNÉE

CHAPTER XV

An Elusive Enemy

In spite of their former experiences the troops under Lord Methuen were in some danger of forgetting the sterner realities of warfare, and of mistaking for them the mere physical discomforts incidental to life afield in rough weather. The camp at Zwaartzkopjesfontein – the highest point of land within a large area – was scattered amongst rocks and boulders piled high into an island ridge rising from the plain; and amongst the rocks and ferns one found here and there a piece of lawn (long untrodden by any feet but those of goats) large enough to picket one's horses and pitch one's tent upon. Eastward the plain stretched to the horizon, as level as the sea; indeed, in a landscape so monotonous that one was fain to decorate it with fancies, it stood for the sea, and touched the rocky base of our island as the sea washes many a mile of bluff coast. Winter was setting in, and all day long wreaths of mist and banks of rain came blowing from the eastward (the seaward, as we called it), and shrouded the brown rock. The signallers on the height used to wrap themselves in their oilskins as darkness fell and lamps took the place of flags and spy-glasses; in the dark gusty hours we heard the "all's well" of a sentry as the visiting patrol went by, much as one hears the cry of the watch on board ship; and down below, the mimosa-trees sighed like surges against the foot of the rock.

The ten days spent there by the troops were marked by only two expeditions against the invisible enemy, neither of which achieved anything but a nominal result. One was under Colonel Mahon, and repaired the telegraph line in the neighbourhood of Modder River; it was intended to patrol as far as Klip Drift, but the rain made the veldt impassable for waggons. Certainly the line was repaired, but, as the Colonel contemptuously remarked, "What's the use of sending an expedition to repair telegraph lines? An old woman can cut 'em again ten minutes after you've gone."

The other flying column was under General Douglas, and was sent out eastward in search of a commando known to be in the neighbourhood. As both columns started on the same day (April 11th) I could not be with both, so I chose General Douglas's as offering the better chances of an engagement. Two days before Lord Chesham had conducted a reconnaissance with his cavalry, to which I had been invited, and at which he had promised me "fine sport." Result: a fine cross-country gallop, a deal of used-up horseflesh, a number of tired and (because they had been hurried out without their breakfasts) rather cross men, and a sight of a few Boers riding off at a distance of five miles. "Butterflies" was someone's description of these elusive enemies of ours; and when one considers what a fine chase they gave us, and how hot and cross we became in the course of it, the description seems not inapt.

General Douglas's column, consisting of a battalion of the Northamptons, 300 Imperial Yeomanry, 50 men of the Kimberley Mounted Corps, a section of Field Artillery, Ambulance and Supply Corps, set out before dawn on Wednesday, April 11th. We marched, as it had hitherto been my lot always to march in this campaign, eastwards towards the fires of dawn, leaving the dark night-sky behind us. The waggons creaked and jolted across the rough veldt, the gun harness jingled, the horses snorted out the cold air, the Kaffirs cried to their beasts; and in this discordant chorus we stretched out across the sea-plain while the east kindled and glowed. Above us the clouds changed from grey to dove-colour, from that to rose-pink; and then, straight before us, the sun came up and gave us gold for redness. The little purple wild flowers opened, showing us where the night had left a jewel on every petal, and the sleepy soldiers plucked them as they passed and cheered themselves with their faint fragrance. The day, like the night, comes quickly there, and brings with it an even greater change. For in that last week of autumn we tasted of every season; hot summer days, nights of spring, dark, cold winter mornings by the camp fire; and it was when night changed to day that winter faded into summer. For that reason, I suppose, the hour after sunrise was the most invigorating of all, and long before the sun had dried the dew from their clothes the men were marching with a freer step.

This will show you how suddenly things may come upon the unwary in that country. I had been riding with the scouts, two miles in advance of the column, and we had just been examining through glasses a moving group in the distance. It turned out to be nothing but cattle feeding – the only moving things in a plain that seemed absolutely level, and I rode back and rejoined the column. The Brigadier was just saying that he was afraid we should see nothing to-day, when an orderly galloped up with a note from Lord Chesham (who was out with the scouts on our left flank) to say that the Boers were holding a kopje three miles on our left front in strength.

Then began the excitement. Everyone was wide awake in a moment and curious to see how the new Brigadier would manage his first job. The convoy was halted, and the troops drawn on under cover of a slight and almost imperceptible rise in the ground. Riding on in advance I suddenly came on the scouts in action, that is to say, their horses were picketed in rear of them, and they were lying hidden in the long grasses. And there you have a typical picture of this kind of warfare. A row of men lying on the ground, for no apparent reason, chewing the long stalks and talking quietly to each other; in front a flat and seemingly vacant ground; profound silence reigning everywhere. But use your glasses, and you will see what looks like a shadow, but is really a rise on the ground, giving advantage enough for the extermination of an army; show your head, and you will hear the bang and whirr of the Mauser.

Presently the jingle of harness sounded behind me, and the guns went by to take up a position on the left. I followed behind them in shelter of the ridge, and therefore out of sight of the position. When I saw it again I found that we were facing three long low mounds, running north and south across our path, and the attack was now being developed. The infantry, so dense a mass when marching, were now strung out in long lines sweeping towards the left, and Lord Chesham with two squadrons had also gone far to the left, to try to get round the position. Meanwhile the guns were unlimbered, and their anxious crew (the battery had never been in action before) were on tenter-hooks.

Up rides a staff officer. "Shell that ridge on the left."

"Right, sir. Sight for 1,800. Fuse six – no, six and a half," says the nervous subaltern.

"Fire, number one gun! Fire, number two gun!" Then two shattering explosions, the suspense of six seconds, the burst of shrapnel in the air, the cloud of brown dust rising where it struck, and the hollow "boom" coming back when all was over.

These exercises were repeated with much zeal by the subaltern and his crew, until after about fifty rounds had been fired the order came to cease fire; and it was afterwards ascertained that, as the net result of this commotion, one partridge had been shot. But I know of another result. A certain subaltern member of the Royal Regiment of Artillery sat thereafter a little straighter on his horse than he had sat a week ago.

But while the noise was going on, for all we knew, the Boers might be suffering heavily from the shrapnel; although we rather thought not, since no one was shooting back at the guns. Meanwhile the infantry was threading out to the left, from which direction a shot now and then sounded; and the remark of the onlookers (the onlooker is invariably a critic) was, "Why is he committing all his force to a left-flank turning movement, leaving only a hundred and fifty men to watch his centre and right, when there may be only a dozen men on that left kopje?"

So said we, who sat on the gun limbers looking very wise; and, by one of those unfortunate chances which sometimes justify the amateur critic and encourage him in his vice, we turned out to be right. What was really happening was this. The 150 or 400 Boers (I never discovered which, although I believe it was the smaller number) who sat on that hill and saw us coming did not wish to stay. So they held the middle kopje, and threw out what is called a "false flank" on to the left kopje; and then, seeing our whole force committed to the left, they went behind the hill and filled their pipes, and packed their saddlebags and rode off, leaving the six men to keep us busy while they went. And then the six men departed also; and after much careful scouting, we rode victoriously over the kopje. If we had attacked on the right flank also, we should probably have caught them, as Lord Chesham would in a little longer have got round to their rear and cut them off. Of course, the whole difficulty in such cases arises from the invisible fire of smokeless powder. One never knows whether the banging is produced by six men firing briskly or by sixty firing slowly, and that was why Lord Chesham had to tire out his horses by taking them round twelve miles to avoid six men.

Our only "casualty" was carried out of action in a stretcher – he was a member of the volunteer company of the Northamptons.

"They've got me, sir," he said to me, in tones of mingled pride and martyrdom, "'it in the leg."

As a matter of fact, the man was only scratched; he could easily walk, but could not resist the circumstance of the stretcher; and he fell into his place for the rest of the march, a very proud man.

We bivouacked at Granaatz Plaatz farm that night, whence the heliograph winked the news of our engagement to our camp. It was a day of alternate sunshine and cloud, and the messages gave the signallers much trouble. I had one to send after the official messages, and the sun was getting low by the time it began. The shine never lasted for more than twenty seconds, but they managed to edge the words into the blinks until they came to "Zwaartzkopjesfontein." The sun always gave out in the middle of it; the regulations demanded that the word should be begun afresh every time, and finally the sun sank victoriously on the fell word. Darkness set in, and a blinding thunderstorm with deluges of rain, but the signallers were not to be beaten.

"We'll do ut on the lamp, sorr, and divil take the ould sun for goin' out on us," said the Irish sergeant.

I should not like to say how many people had to do with that message before it got near the cable. In the first place, the light could hardly penetrate the twelve-mile space of rain; and even when they had succeeded in "calling up" headquarters the lightning flashes interfered with our feeble dots and dashes. I shall always remember that little group of men working most admirably on the kopje high up amid the storm and rain – one lying on his face in the mud with a telescope propped on a stone reading the reply; another keeping the paper dry under his helmet while he spelt the message to the operator; and a third working the shutter that, by occulting the light, makes flashes from the lamp.

"*Guardian* – G-u-a-r-d-i-a-n," says the reader.

"Bang, bang; rattle; bang, rattle, rattle; bang; bang, bang, rattle; bang, rattle; bang, rattle, rattle; bang, bang, bang," goes the lamp.

An anxious pause is enlivened by a clap of thunder.

"Answered," says Spy-glass. And often a word had to be repeated three or four times before it was answered, but at the fourth letter of "Zwaartzkopjesfontein" the answering signal was plainly given, followed by DDDD, which, although not in the code-book, is an expression well understood by all signallers.

All that night it rained, and the men in their wretched bivouacs sang through it all with a most admirable heroism. Imagine yourself with two other people lying in three inches of water with two blankets supported by rifles over your head, and you have their condition. And they started again in the cold, rainy darkness, wet and chilled to the bone, still singing. But that is the private soldier all over. Put him in really happy circumstances, and he grumbles himself hoarse; give him something really to grumble at, and he is cheerful; give him misery, and he sings. We marched fifteen miles on Thursday, the 12th, and encamped at Buitendam, the farm of a field-cornet, where a few of the enemy sniped at us as we arrived and had the satisfaction of seeing the whole force turned out after a weary march. But of course the Boers are in their element at this kind of game. A hundred of them wish to drive away some stock; they leave a dozen to snipe from a ridge, while we send Tommy plodding round for miles on a flanking movement (for you must keep him out of range); and when the cattle have been driven far enough away, Mr. Boer jumps on his horse and is off also, while we ruefully "occupy" the vacant hill.

We found a noisy and rather gratifying revenge in destroying some ammunition which was buried in the garden; the throwing of three thousand rounds of cordite ammunition into the fire is a peculiarly exciting game. Some presiding genius, instead of blowing up the two cases of dynamite, threw them into the dam, whence, I have been told, they were fished up, not a penny the worse, by the Boers after our departure next day.

A thing happened in connection with this Boer ammunition which shows once more how very easy it is to attribute all kinds of sins to one's enemy. Someone came running up to a little group of us with several packets of cartridges, one with the seal broken.

"Here's a pretty thing," he said; "poisoned bullets – the brutes!"

Sure enough, there were the steel bullets projecting out of the cartridges, each completely coated with something very like verdigris up to the edge of the brass envelope. The sealed packets showed that they must have been so received from the makers, which easily proved the most premeditated barbarity. Exclamations were rife; a brigadier was making notes in his pocket-book; someone was urging a correspondent to send home a cable announcing the fact, when a man, who had been sitting quietly through it all, said –

"That's all very well, but how about the rifling in the barrel? I guess there wouldn't be much of that stuff left on by the time the bullet was spinning."

Silence fell like a cloud on the group, and the bubble was finally pricked when another officer came up and said –

"More bad grease! I've had to chuck out half a box of ammunition because the grease has gone bad and fouls the rifles."

Of course; it was as simple as day. The bullets had, as usual, been dipped in grease to preserve them, and the grease had gone bad. When I returned to the little circle there was an animated conversation in progress on the subject of visiting patrols.

We marched in next day, eighteen miles, having covered a pear-shaped track eastwards of about forty miles, while the men behaved like Trojans under most uncomfortable circumstances.

We remained for some days in camp, waiting for Lord Roberts to move, and fighting no more dangerous enemy than the wet and boisterous weather of young winter. Certainly Lord Methuen had a fine force there, well tried and in excellent condition, and we all hoped that he might be given a chance to do something with it. There is something at once lonely and lofty in the position of a General Officer in the field that wins one's sympathy. You see it most plainly at a full church parade such as was held on Easter Sunday, when the whole force was formed into a hollow square. Walls of living faces; before them, a few paces, company officers; before them again, commanding officers; the chaplain in the middle; and then the pleasant-looking Guardsman striding into his place in front of all and saluting the chaplain – the only person to whom that honour is rendered. After the short service the General's position is still more sharply indicated, when the shouting of orders takes the place of the parson's placid tones.

"Northamptons! *'shon!* Fours left, by the left – quick – *march!*" and the tramp of feet nears the spot where the General stands alone. Down the whole battalion you hear the order run, "Company! eyes *left!*" and hundreds of eyes are turned on the General, until the (to him) welcome "Eyes *front!*" relieves him from so particular a scrutiny. Is it not a paragon of what he has to endure from the world?

CHAPTER XVI

A Surprise on the March

Strangely enough, I had just written the last chapter, describing the profound peace of our environments, when from my tent near the farmhouse I saw one after another of the headquarters staff mount their horses and gallop westwards up the hill after Lord Methuen, who was easily first. One learns to read signs quickly in a military camp, and it did not require much intuition to understand that something was, in the phrase of the orderly at the vacant headquarters, "bloomin' well hup." My own horse was ready in five minutes, and when I reached the top of the hill I found the cavalry horse lines vacant.

The site of the Zwaartzkopjesfontein camp turns an abrupt face eastwards, but on the westward side the plateau slopes almost imperceptibly to the plain, which is, in its immediate neighbourhood, thickly sown with kopjes. Down this slope the cavalry were galloping, about two miles in advance of me, in squadron formation, towards a small kopje on which we had a picket. Realising that nothing could happen immediately, I followed them at a foot-pace, and came up with them at the foot of the hill where they had dismounted. Scouts were sent out westwards among the low bush with which these slopes are clothed, and from the top of the hill one could see them scattering and spreading over ten miles of country; but no sound broke the silence of the hills. Summer was back again to-day; our sea-plain was calm, shimmering in the haze; and only the buzz of an insect disturbed the peace of the little group on the brown hill.

While we were watching the scouts I heard what was in the wind. It seemed that an outpost of four yeomen, who were stationed about six miles north-west from camp, had so far forgotten the delicacy of their position as to light a fire and cook a turkey which they had found. They were surprised in the act by a small party of Boers, who fired upon them. Of the men thus surprised three were taken unhurt, while the fourth escaped slightly wounded, and, returning to camp, told the disturbing tale. Three squadrons had instantly been turned out to attempt a rescue, and it was on their heels that I had come out. We waited for an hour, and then the scouts came in one by one, all with the same tale. Nothing to be seen – no Boers; one thought that he had seen two on the sky line seven miles away, but they might have been Kaffirs rounding up cattle – he was not sure. So we had to give up the men for lost, and ride back to camp in a hurry and in rather bad temper, for it was mail day, and time was precious. But the little disaster proved to be a cheap enough lesson to the Yeomanry, and also to be the herald of operations far more important.

This happened on Thursday, April 19th. On Friday morning I was out at the same place at half-past six, because a staff officer had told me the night before that there was "a show on," and a "show" may mean anything from a patrol to a reconnaissance in force. Lord Chesham, who was in command, was sitting on the kopje with his staff, and I climbed up and joined them, the cavalry remaining as before underneath the hill while the scouts went out. We sat for an hour, comparing each other's glasses, until the stones became hotter and hotter and the sky line began to wave in the heat. At last I rode out to where there was an advanced picket, and sat searching the horizon with glasses. We were in a little grove of mimosa, and the doves were busy above our heads. After waiting for another hour we saw some Boers to the north, and presently the right flank scouts came in to report that there were about forty Boers working northwards on our flank.

That was quite enough. Everyone was back at the kopje in no time, and Lord Chesham sent out Lord Scarborough with one squadron, and Colonel Mahon with another.

I went with Lord Scarborough's. We rode out to the point at which the picket had been cut off, and saw more and more Boers coming from the north – about seventy – but they never got within range, although they worked closer and closer. Our little body of men was so well protected by flankers and scouts that, when the Boers at length began to steal along our flank with the evident intention of sniping us as we returned, we were able to retire before they came within range, having discovered the very useful fact that they were becoming more numerous and bolder in our neighbourhood.

As we passed through the camp we saw waggons and tents being packed. Advancing at last? Oh, dear, no. Only Lord Kitchener at the other end of the wire playing with us again. We were to retire on Boshof, but Lord Methuen decided, instead of going into the town, to encamp at Beck's Farm about five miles out, where the grazing was better. The lay mind found it hard to understand the purpose of these movements. Lord Methuen had been humbugged and baffled by Headquarters in what seemed at the time a most unbusinesslike way. First he was ordered out from Kimberley to Griquatown. When he was there and had 400 Boers in his grasp he received a message ordering him back to Kimberley at once. Then he was sent to Boshof and ordered to march with all speed on Hoopstad. Having reached Mahemsfontein he was ordered to halt, and that place being unsuitable for an encampment, had to fall back on Zwaartzkopjesfontein. And then he was ordered back to Boshof again. No doubt the explanation was that the advance of the main army under Lord Roberts had been delayed, but of course the Boers believed that all this was due to their own formidable movements, and were accordingly encouraged.

Well, there was no doubt that we were moving, and I hoped that we were going to march in the direction of Fourteen Streams and do something towards the relief of Mafeking. That was what we had all been longing to do, and it was with a long face that a staff officer said, "Back to Boshof."

So back we started.

Our column was nearly three miles long, and just as the tail of it was leaving camp and the head of it, like a snake's, beginning to curl round Spitz Kop – a lofty cone-shaped kopje beside the road – pom – pom – pom – pom! suddenly sounded from – where? The wicked little shells licked like a rising tide along our right flank.

Up on a ridge far on our right I saw the rogues working their gun, as busy as monkeys. Our friend the pom-pom once more, and most vivacious. At the same time I heard the banging of Mausers behind me, and the air above sang for an instant. And when that flight was over – Boom...! and the long screaming whirr – sounds which tell you that someone has touched off a field-gun, and that the shell is coming your way. This one was a common shell, and did not come within a hundred yards. The whole thing was very prettily done. Such a surprise, too. We had no idea that they had guns.

Turning my horse round I paused for an instant to watch the effect and the result. The column was still moving on, the Kaffir drivers shouting a little louder than usual perhaps, but not a bullock out of place or even a sheep touched. They were firing on a rather vulnerable part of the convoy, where a flock of about a thousand sheep were being driven and the remount horses led. But even while I looked the rear-guard was spreading out and joining hands with the right flank, and the sound of rifle fire from the ridge showed that they were already engaged. The pom-pom and the 12-pounder continued for about a quarter of an hour, and then our battery opened with a roar and silenced them in about two minutes. And all the while the convoy jolted along the road, and the rest of the action, or the chief part of it, remained with the right flank. But I could see the Boers galloping along the ridge in front of us to be ready for the convoy when it should come up, and certainly that ought not to have been possible. It is ungrateful to criticise the Yeomanry who had been doing so very well and learning so quickly, but, if the truth must be told, their work on the right flank that day was not beyond reproach. Once, when the fire was slack, I went across to the right, and rode back very quickly, for I found kopjes which, according to all military rules, should have been occupied by us, held by the enemy.

Of course to guard efficiently the flank of a marching column is not easy for untried troops, especially when a running fight has to be kept up. In this kind of country, where a line of kopjes runs parallel with the road, the best plan is for two flanking parties to occupy them by turn. Thus A party should occupy No. 1 kopje and B party No. 2; when No. 1 needs no longer to be held A leaves it and seizes No. 3, and then B leaves No. 2 and occupies No. 4, and so on. But the Yeomanry were strolling aimlessly along the foot of the kopjes, while the nimble Boer was climbing up the other side to the top, and shooting down upon them – or over their heads at the convoy – as he pleased.

It is a marvel that of our twenty casualties only two were killed. If the Boers had known of our movement just a little sooner I fear we should have suffered heavily, or at least lost many cattle and perhaps a few waggons. At the same time we were taken at the usual disadvantage of a moving force that has to defend itself, and, with the exception of the flanking, our work was done really well. The guns at once silenced the Boer artillery, and they were brought into action so expeditiously that the Boers never got the proper range. It is true that one shell plumped into the middle of a flock of sheep, but I believe it killed only two. And our rear-guard fought manfully. The fire was heavy there, and one could not see much, but I saw enough to realise that theirs was stiff work. They and darkness finished the engagement, and we went on to Boshof, arriving there just as night closed in.

I shall never forget riding down the main street in pitch darkness – the street full of waggons (each with its sixteen oxen), blundering about, the waggon in front of one suddenly stopping, and the waggon behind coming on – cries, curses, hailings, and railings of the drivers and soldiers – everyone trying to find his camp or his waggons or his horses, and not a light to be seen. And, in spite of it all, order emerged from the chaos; brigade signals flashing, camps pitched, pickets posted to keep watch over us all night, fires lighted, stations allotted; and presently "last post" and "lights out," and in spite of the bellowing oxen, rest.

CHAPTER XVII

Under the Red Cross Flag

There was a burial party going out to Spitz Kop early the next morning, and Major Pollock and I had leave to go with it. No one was armed, the ambulance being preceded by an orderly carrying the P.M.O.'s bath-towel. When we came near to the Boer pickets we rode on with the bath-towel, while the Red Cross flag waved over the ambulance; and had come quite close before we distinguished the two figures sitting amongst the large brown boulders of the hill.

They both spoke English and treated us with civility. They were both farmers from the neighbourhood of Boshof, and had a keen appetite for news of the town. We were soon deep in an examination of their weapons – one of them had a beautiful Mauser sporting rifle, hair-sighted, of which he was extremely proud; altogether we had quite a friendly chat. They gave us the best information they could as to the whereabouts of our dead and wounded, but it seemed that the Boer ambulance party had been out working all night, and had recovered nearly all the wounded as well as the bodies of two dead.

We went on behind the kopje into a level space surrounded by ridges, and as we advanced (the bath-towel well to the fore) mounted men began to appear from behind the ridges. First by twos and threes, then by sixes and dozens, from north and south and east and west the black figures came cantering towards us, until our little party was surrounded by, I suppose, three or four hundred mounted men. The babel of talk was deafening; everyone had something to say about the fight of yesterday; and in addition to that it was easily apparent that merely as Englishmen we were objects of absorbing interest to these pastoral Free Staters. I know that my tobacco-pouch was empty in about two minutes, and I presently fell into more particular conversation with the Boer doctor, who had been up all night attending to his own and our wounded. It was a rough-and-ready kind of first aid that he gave; a whisky-bottle filled with carbolic dressing hung from his saddle on one side, and on the other were rolls of lint and bandages; but I believe that the ambulance equipment in the laager was thoroughly complete. He told me of one of our men who had been wounded in the thigh, and had been seen late the night before crawling about on the ground; but when they had brought back a stretcher for him they had not been able to find him. The doctor thought he knew where he was likely to be, so I

84

volunteered to go with him and search the place. The doctor and I, therefore, with one other Boer, rode away towards the west.

The wind was blowing strong from the west, choking down our voices as we tried to speak while we rode; and therefore we had no idea until some hours later of the excitement that was caused by our departure. It seemed that the Commandant, who had been engaged in conversation with our doctor, had ordered that no one should advance any farther into the Boer position, and that the empty ambulances must be sent on to receive the dead and wounded. Indeed we heard afterwards that the friendly outpost which we first encountered had got into very hot water for allowing us to pass. When I galloped off, therefore, I was unconsciously disobeying a very important order, and several of the Boers and our own party shouted after me that I must come back; but riding against a stiff breeze none of us could hear a word, and we were so soon out of sight and over the ridge that the Boers, with a shrug, left me to my fate. Pollock called the second in command (a Scotchman, I regret to say) to witness that I had not heard the order, and he promised to intercede on my behalf with the Commandant, who was a son of General Cronje of Paardeberg fame.

I had now better return to my own adventures. With my two companions I soon reached a rocky plateau, where the horses had to choose their steps carefully amongst the sharp stones, and searching thus for about an hour we had a long and interesting conversation. I remember asking one of them what his real feeling was about their chance of success.

"We shall win," he said, with that simple confidence, born of ignorance and self-trust, which is often a dangerous element in a force opposed to us. "Lord Roberts with all his army cannot leave Bloemfontein; we oppose him there. Your Lord Methuen cannot advance here; he has had to retire twice."

We knew that they would thus interpret Lord Roberts's delay and his contradictory orders to Lord Methuen, but it was rather galling not to be able to deny it.

"We have no dislike for the English," the man went on; and it was at least true of him and many of the Free Staters whom I met, although it was not true of all the Transvaalers. "You are brave soldiers and you fight well and we can respect you, but you are led astray by Joe Chamberlain." His face darkened when he uttered the name; I had a glimpse of a man hated by a nation.

"Rhodes, too," he said, but with less hatred and more contempt. "If we had caught him in Kimberley we should have killed him, but if *we* don't kill him----" and he named an alternative in which he clearly saw a Providence working on behalf of the wronged.

I asked him a little later what he thought of our generals and of whom he was most afraid? He was quite ready with an opinion.

"There is no difference," he said, with a lofty air, "it makes no difference to us; we take them as they come. First come first served." He was even impartial. "Your Lord Methuen has been blamed for Magersfontein, but the English do not know that we were as much surprised and scared as he was when his troops stumbled on us in the dark. It was a very near thing for us. We are not afraid of Kitchener of whom you talk so much. Roberts? Yes, he is a fairly good general, but alone we do not fear him. Roberts and Kitchener together are good; we do not like them. But alone we will take them on any day."

Although we talked for a long time I did not really learn much from these Boers, who represented the most unthinking class. Just as I had found the English colonists to conduct their arguments in a circle and constantly to bring forward the same old statements, so I found these Boers repeating the same assertions over and over again: that the Lord was on their side; that they must prevail in the end; that they could not trust us; that we had played them false; that we were really after their gold-fields; "if there had been no gold in South Africa there would have been no war." They spoke as men who repeated a lesson; yet I am bound to say that they spoke with sincerity, and although they seemed to speak parrot-wise, they probably accepted current forms of speech as giving the best expression to a deep and universal conviction.

We had been riding for nearly two hours, when one of my companions noticed marks on the ground evidently made by a man dragging himself along. We followed this spoor down the rocky slope where ferns and little shrubs divided the stones. It wound about, choosing the smoothest places, covering altogether a distance of about a mile; it led us at last to the shade of a mimosa bush, where the poor soldier had ended his duty and journey together.

There was nothing to be done now but to rejoin my party, and when I expressed a wish to do so the doctor said, "This will be your nearest way," pointing to a barrier range of low hills. They lay in the right direction, so I rode on for about a mile and a half, the two Boers still accompanying me, until we reached the top of the nearest hill. What was my surprise to see lying below me the smoke and waggons and picketed horses of the enemy's laager! The Boers, to the number of perhaps seven or eight hundred, were sitting or lying beneath trees that made a circle round the mile-wide basin. I glanced at the faces of my companions with some misgiving, but honesty was written there.

"I have no business to be here, you know," said I. "We shall all get into a row." They preceded me down the slope, and, with a presentiment that I should get out again, I slipped out my pocket compass and made a mental note of the bearings of the laager from Spitz Kop, the head of which was visible about six miles away. There was a small farmhouse which appeared to be used as headquarters; round this were twenty or thirty waggons piled with cases, but, so far as I could see, no forage or oats. There were either three or four guns; there were certainly four gun-carriages, but one of them may have been a limber. As we came into the basin a small, young-looking man, to whom I was introduced as the Commandant, met us.

"Please remain here," he said to me sharply; and as he led the doctor away, pouring forth a stream of Dutch, I gathered that my poor friend was getting into trouble. At last Cronje came back and addressed me, speaking English very imperfectly. This is the substance of what he said –

"You should never have been allowed to come here, and it is my duty to detain you as a prisoner."

I remonstrated. "I'm a non-combatant, sir."

"I cannot help that. You are here and you have seen this place, and I must send you to Pretoria, whence, if the authorities are satisfied that you are a genuine non-combatant, you may be sent to Delagoa Bay. It was very foolish of you to come here."

I explained that I had come in ignorance, not knowing where my guide would lead me; that I had come to look for a wounded man, and under the protection of a flag of truce; that the whole thing was an unfortunate accident, and that he should treat it as such.

Much to my surprise he seemed to waver. "If I were to let you go" – and he looked at me sideways – "would you undertake to give no information?"

I suggested that the question was an unfair one. "You know how you would answer it yourself, sir."

"Yes" (he was melting), "we are honourable also, and to our own side first of all. I have spoken of you with the doctor," he said, looking at me kindly for the first time, "and I shall let you go. By rights you ought to go to Pretoria. Of course your general may come and attack us here, and your information will be useful, but we are strong enough for all the English. Bring his horse," he shouted to someone standing by, and to me, "You may go. No, you may not!" he added sharply; and then, with a smile, "not until you have had a cup of coffee."

Upon this civility we parted, but it was not until I had rejoined my anxious friends with the ambulance that I began to suspect Commandant Cronje of a piece of pleasantry. Major Pollock, it appeared, had interceded on my behalf so effectually that my fate had been decided and my safe return promised long before I had met the Commandant. He afterwards entertained himself by playing upon my anxiety, which, I have no doubt, was apparent enough.

But now the ambulance was slowly returning from the place whither it had been sent to receive the dead bodies. A place for the grave was chosen where a thorn tree spread shadows on the ground. There were stony hills all round, encircling a wide and green basin just within the Boer lines, and it was beside one of these that the grave was dug. The ground was very hard and the labour severe; it was at least two hours before the fatigue-party, working in short shifts, had excavated a resting-place for the two bodies. While they were working the Boers gathered round us to the number of a couple of hundred. They were very silent, eyeing us with an absorbed interest that embraced every article of our equipment. Men of the humblest peasant class, poorly – in many respects wretchedly – clad, they presented, in their ragged and shabby apparel, a sharp contrast to our Yeomanry soldiers, who seemed, by comparison, trim and well cared for. The Boers wore their ordinary clothes, which were relieved by only one military touch – the bandolier. This was generally of home manufacture, and in many cases was a touching and significant document of affection. "Thought flies best when the hands are easily busy"; ah, how many thoughts and fears had been worked into those bandoliers when busy fingers wrought them in the far-away farmhouse! In some of them, I thought, portraits of the makers were to be discovered. Fancy stitches and cunning invention which provided for thrice the usual number of cartridges told one tale; flannel paddings which sought to make of the military appointment a winter garment told another. The Boers, I suppose, envied us our serge and whipcord, but to examine their homely makeshifts was to realise that even the art of Stohwasser may leave something to be desired. Although they eyed us diligently they had now fallen strangely silent; they offered us little conversation, but spoke freely in low tones amongst themselves; they replied to our questions with a brief civility that did not encourage any very brisk intercourse. We soon gave up the attempt and lay down under the shade of the ambulance in our sheltered hollow, listening to the wind singing in the thin vegetation of the hill above us.

The sound of picks ceased at last, and an orderly came to report that the grave was ready. The stretchers were withdrawn from the ambulance and exposed two bodies stained with soil and blood – one shot through the lungs, another through the head; neither of them remarkable for the dignity that death is supposed to lend to the meanest features, both looking strangely small and almost grotesque in their crumpled postures: two troopers of the Yeomanry, known (as it happened) to not one man of the crowd; and now emerging, before they reached a final obscurity, to be for a moment a mark for all our thoughts and eyes. They were laid beside the grave; the Boers ranked themselves upon one side, we upon the other; the doctor opened his book and, shyly enough, began the service. A bird flew twittering and perched on the thorn above us, making the office choral.

You are to remember that there were present to us just the simplest facts of life. Hills and the naked sun, great winds and death – before these we may cease to make believe; they tune and temper us to accordance with pulses which, if only we are honest, will give us back multiplied our own faintest vibration. Honesty is easy when we can forget ourselves; and here, where the wind seemed to pluck the words from the reader's mouth and carry them to the hills that matched them in grandeur, they cut the last link between us and our selfish thoughts and fears, imparting a sense of world-without-end, making us one with our feathered clerk who, his red-brown wings folded, wove a thread of song into the Psalm. In that texture of admonition and prayer are many seizing pictures: man walking in a vain shadow and disquieting himself in vain, heaping up riches, ignorant who shall gather them: man turned to destruction: our secret sins set in the light of one countenance: a displeasure in which we consume away: a wrathful indignation that can make all our busy years as a tale that is told. The first thought in each of us had been, "There, but for the grace of God, I lie"; but the bird's song seemed so to chase away all shadows of self-pity that Death appeared in his natural order with the wind and rain and sun; no more unkind than they.

At a signal the bodies were placed in the earth. No hateful furniture; clay against clay: they seemed almost to nestle in it. A trooper covered one face with his handkerchief, his comrade shielded the other with a branch of mimosa; and while the words flowed to an end we stood, Dutchmen and Englishmen, our small quarrel for the moment forgotten, face to face with clear truth and knowing for once the taste of sincerity. It was a good prayer to pray, that at our own last hour we should not fall from that charity for any pains of death.

It seemed a natural thing for us to shake hands with the Boers before we turned to resume this game of hostility in which we stumbled upon such great issues. It was a silent ride home, and I need not say that it went sore against the grain with me to make my report to Lord Methuen and the Intelligence Department respecting the position of the laager. My thoughts were not upon compass bearings and distances, but in the sun-steeped basin where the grave was; and all day long I had a picture in my mind of two groups of men united in one human emotion, but now seeking each others' lives. At night, long after the camp slept, I lay awake with the echo of the graveside "last post" ringing in my ears, and, because of the appetite for effect that afflicts us in weak moments, I was teased and worried by a sense of incompleteness. In a military camp, after "last post" and "lights out" have been sounded, no bugle save that which sounds an alarm may be blown until the hour of reveille. The soldiers under the hill had been trumpeted to their last sleep; in a few hours I should hear the morning call: why should they never hear it again? Suddenly my irrational complaint was silenced as certain words of Saint Paul to the Corinthians reverberated in my mind. After all, it was well; one night was but a little longer than the other; and, those words being true, my troopers should wake to a familiar sound.

PART V

With the Flying Column to Mafeking

CHAPTER XVIII

A Strategic Secret

It was now more than six weeks since we had hurried from Bloemfontein to be in time for the expected operations for the relief of Mafeking. When Lord Methuen had moved from Boshof we had been sure that Mafeking was the goal, and I think that Lord Methuen himself had at least expected to conduct a turning movement on the Boer position at Fourteen Streams. It is easy to see now, when even Lord Roberts's strong march on Pretoria has been harassed and his communications interrupted, why such a movement of Methuen's small force could not have been successful; but we did not see it then. There was a great dearth of information, and the secret of the Flying Column was kept perfectly until within a few days of its departure. While we were waiting at Boshof in the blank days that followed the rear-guard engagement everyone suspected his fellow of some secret information, and men's most trivial movements were elaborately construed into indications that they meditated some independent action. Even Lord Methuen was so much in the dark that he used to say he liked to see the correspondents coming, as he supposed it meant that he should have something to do. Those of us who were there knew really nothing, and had only come prompted by a vague instinct that something was in the air.

Unavoidable as the delay in despatching a column to the relief of Mafeking seems to have been, I think that there was one moment at which, if Lord Methuen had had a slightly stronger force under his command, the course of the campaign on the north-west frontier might have been changed, and Mafeking relieved by pressure from the south. After my accidental discovery of the Boer laager near Spitz Kop there was a long discussion by Lord Methuen and his staff of the possibilities of surrounding and attacking the enemy. It was plain that this large force, commanded by young Cronje, had moved across from Fourteen Streams with the object of harrying us and perhaps retaking Boshof; and for a few days there was practically no force at Fourteen Streams. Now if Lord Methuen could have sent out a light column westward from Boshof to the rear of the laager, and also held the enemy in front with the remainder of his force, he might with good fortune have bagged the whole Boer force, which he knew from my information to be weak in guns. I know he was urged to do it; I know he wanted to do it; I know what the chance of a sensational success meant to a man whose successes had hitherto been unexciting and his one failure a spectacle; and I admired him for not running the risk. It would have been so easy to yield to the urgency of his staff and Intelligence Department, and success was almost certainly assured; but Lord Methuen, who has been foolishly accused of all kinds of rashness, chose in this case to read in that "almost" an assurance that he was not justified in taking the risk. He had no Horse Artillery; and the rapid and secret march to the rear of the laager might have been impossible with field-guns. So he decided at any rate; and decisions like these are among not the least important victories of a campaign.

Since the Boers were in the neighbourhood, and might at any moment make an attack, Major Pollock and I were anxious not to leave Boshof until it became absolutely necessary. We had a secret agent watching our interests at Kimberley in the person of a staff officer whose name I suppose I had better not mention; thus we witnessed, without misgiving, the sudden and hurried flight of all the other correspondents from Boshof, mystery written on their faces. Thus we spent two more peaceful days riding in the shady lanes and lying on the sunburnt kopjes, sweeping the horizon with the telescopes of Lord Chesham and his pleasant crew; thus we received a telegram from Kimberley advising us to "come here and attend to the business yourselves"; thus we rode away and closed what will remain in my memory as the pleasantest chapter in the campaign.

The diary that follows was written during the march of the Relief Column – not always under the most favourable circumstances. The imperfections of a document of this kind are so closely bound up with its only merit that I have decided to leave it exactly as it was written, and not to risk a sacrifice of reality in an attempt to abolish defects which, I hope, the reader will regard as being in the circumstances unavoidable.

CHAPTER XIX

The Departure From Kimberley

BARKLY WEST, *Thursday, May 3rd.*

At last!

During the inaction of the past weeks there has been but one question asked – "Is nothing to be done for Mafeking?" With the gallant little garrison waiting and keeping the enemy from the door while disease is busy within, it has been hard to sit still and wait for the orders that have been so long in coming. But Kimberley, which had been almost emptied of troops by Lord Methuen's departure, gradually filled again as General Hunter's division assembled; and a few days ago it became plain that some movement was imminent.

Tuesday evening – the eve of the mysterious move – was full of romance for anyone who knew what was about to happen. The dining-room of the club was gay with yellow and brass and scarlet and the subtler colours of wine and flowers; but conversation grouped itself into the small low choruses that indicate far more truly than one united sound indicates the presence of some common and thrilling interest. Earlier in the day I had been admitted to a kind of *séance* in the Press Censor's office, where an envelope alluringly marked "secret" had been opened, and its contents read to a "limited number of correspondents of known discretion." Within it was written that a flying column under Colonel Mahon would set out at daybreak on the 4th from Barkly West for the relief of Mafeking; that a certain number of correspondents (of known discretion) would be invited to accompany it; that the estimated time was fifteen days; that no provisions or forage would be supplied; that the correspondents must give their word of honour to divulge nothing until a certain time: to all of which we set our hands and seals, and then departed from the office somewhat impressed. It is characteristic of our Intelligence Department that on leaving the office I was greeted by a Kimberley resident with the remark – "Well, I hear that Mahon is going to make a dash for Mafeking on Friday *viâ* Barkly West; good business!"

So in the evening, although if you had asked point-blank questions you would have been told nothing, the forthcoming dash to the rescue was really the topic. That it is to be the work of the Colonial troops is fair enough, since no one has a better right than they to help their besieged comrades. Therefore the British officer has been for once eclipsed, and the Colonials have had it all their own way. They hovered and bustled about the club all the evening, taking leave of friends and settling affairs. Some of them, one knew, would not return; and the thought never fails to lend a strange kind of solemnity to the eve of a big enterprise. "We're going to have a tough job," Colonel Peakman had said, and men had looked grave for a moment, and then gone on talking and laughing; but the prospect of serious fighting was displeasing to no one. That is always the way; the excitements and not the horrors of a battle are remembered; every man thinks that, though all the rest should fall, he shall stand at the last; a sense of danger in the future is a trumpet-call. And this is a noble part of warfare, to relieve the distressed. A duty to be done at all costs; no questions of how or why, but a clear lead.

There is something in the very words "flying column" to appease the impatient; wings in the air, a swoop upon the victim. But it is merely a bold figure of speech, and means in a case like this a rapid march of twenty miles a day, mules instead of oxen, short rations, starving and ruined horses. These flying cavalry columns and forced marches (the only means by which the slippery Boer is to be cornered) demonstrate to how great an extent this is a campaign of horses. Only the shortest horse rations can be carried, and even at the best, a fortnight's continuous work of this kind will so knock up a good horse that he must have three months' rest before he can be of any further use. So your flying column must start with fat horses, and use up their reserve of flesh, arriving at the end with skeletons. It is dreadful enough to see a good beast, and hundreds of good beasts, starving before your eyes and working hard all the time; but it is only one of the many horrible and necessary accompaniments of a war. What is asked of the horses on an expedition of this kind is that they shall carry a man say twenty-five miles a day on the march, and at the end perhaps carry him another thirty galloping about in a fight; and no animal will stand more than a fortnight of that, even on full rations. So the remount officers have been busy in Kimberley, buying up every animal that looked as though he would last for a fortnight; and the private buyer has been hard put to it to provide for his needs. I was lucky enough in the two hours of yesterday afternoon that were available for the purpose to light upon a cart and team that would carry my load of forage and bully beef; and at 5 p.m. to see the leaders harnessed in for the first time, while my faithful Kaffir groom gathered up the reins with doubt in his eye. Of course the leaders turned round and tried to climb up over the wheelers' heads, but at length they came to an approximate sort of unanimity as to which pair was to lead. Thereafter I had the fearful joy of seeing the equipage set forth at speed down the narrow street. A policeman escaped with his life at one corner, a cripple was snatched from death at another, a nigger was cannoned off at a third – the proprietor of the public menace riding diffidently behind the while, trying to look as though he had no hand in it. But the great thing was that I had got something capable of "flying" with the column, and I was twice hailed on the way out to know whether I would sell the horses.

From Kimberley to Barkly (whither the forces comprising the column had proceeded earlier in the day) the road lies through twenty-five miles of the loneliest veldt; except at the half-way house I did not see a human being all the way. The young moon was up, and threw the earth and sky into sombre night colours – a purple wall of earth meeting the spangled violet of the sky in one long line. For twenty miles of the road there was hardly a sound save the beat of horses' feet; but presently there stole on my ear a kind of music for which one's senses long in this barren country – the murmur of water over stones. It was the Vaal river, running here broad and deep, and making Barkly West a pleasing instead of a dull place. Beside a sharp bend the lights of an inn shone upon the road, promising rest for tired people, whether they had four feet or two; and the promise was fulfilled.

To-day has been given up to horse-buying; the place was like a fair; everyone who owned even the framework of a horse brought it out and offered it for sale; and officers were competing busily for the purchase of any decent animal. I found time to go down and listen to the river – strange sights the water that is flowing so quietly must have passed this morning! For one of our 6-inch siege guns was sent up to Warrenton last night, and opened at daybreak on the Boers at Fourteen Streams. One longs to know something of the result; but the water flows secretly on into more peaceful scenes.

GUNNING'S FARM, *Saturday, May 5th.*

We did not get away until nearly nine yesterday morning, and for the first few miles were much delayed by breakdowns in the transport column. The transport mule is a troublesome creature; sometimes he insists on stopping to pick up grass; always he is reluctant to do merely what is required of him. So although our transport column is supposed to take up only one mile of road, it straggled over a good two miles during Friday's march. The road was very dangerous, winding through narrow passes and thick bush country; therefore the scouting was slow and laborious, and the whole column was halted before every unusually dangerous place. But we met no Boers; and since we desire to proceed very quietly and unostentatiously at first this was fortunate. The column consists of about eleven hundred men of the Kimberley Mounted Corps and the Imperial Light Horse, a mixed company of picked volunteers from the Sixth Fusilier Brigade (representing England, Ireland, Scotland, and Wales), and a four-gun battery of the Royal Horse Artillery, with two pom-poms in addition. Every man is mounted, including the infantry men, who ride on waggons. Yesterday we marched only twelve miles, owing to the difficulties of the ground, but in the evening our business began in earnest. Lights had to be out at eight o'clock, and this morning we marched off at two, no lights or fires being allowed, not even a match for a cigarette. The joys of rising at 1.30 in the cold pitch darkness (for these are winter mornings, in spite of the summer noonday), and of trying to harness a team, and pick up all one's kit, exist only in retrospect, where all troubles fade. The six-hour march this morning was very cold and very tedious; four hours of it were in darkness, and how late the sun seemed to be in rising! But he came punctually, in spite of a mild panic amongst us lest something should have happened to him, and the pageant of his rising was entertainment for the last two hours. Fifteen miles before breakfast and fifteen after lunch – a journey almost too heavy for the second day. Two teams of mules were knocked up, and more will follow if this goes on.

At Spitz Kop, our breakfast outspan, we heard guns in the distance, and from the top of the high hill we could see the little fluffy clouds of smoke, that meant so much to someone, bursting on both sides. There was an alarm that the Boers were coming our way, and the guns were turned out; but it was a false alarm, and the column came on here to Gunning's Farm, where we arrived after dark. Camping in the dark after a thirty-mile march is wild work – such a commotion of hails and calls, such searching for one's camp, and for the watering-place for horses. The hour of lamplight is precious, and I am near the end of it now.

MUCHADIN, *Monday, May 7th.*

A day seldom passes on which one does not receive fresh proof that the world contains foolish people. In the small hours of Sunday morning, when the camp was astir in the darkness, a rifle-shot rang out quite close to me. I could hear the bullet going up like a rocket until the sound was lost. It was the usual thing – some idiot charging his magazine, and forgetting to close the cut-off – with the result that when he snapped his trigger the gun went off. Any good result of our discomfortable regulation as to fires and lights is quite cancelled by such an act, which proves much more certainly than fires can prove the presence of armed troops. The same thing happened early this morning, and the pickets were turned out to find that the alarm was false. It is a great pity, but where the British soldier is to be found in any force, there seems invariably to be found also the man who lets off his gun by mistake. The marvel is that the thing generally hurts no one.

Sunday's march was uneventful, except that trouble began among the horses. One of my four fellow-correspondents lost a fine pair – the wheelers of his team – which he had bought in Barkly on Thursday, and which probably returned to their former owner. But as we have no lines of communication, he will not see them again. My horse fell sick, and the three hours of the midday bivouac had to be spent in hastily breaking in to the saddle one of the leaders of my team. The headquarters staff lost two horses, and five mules strayed from the supply park. The fact was rather tersely announced by Corporal Jenkins of the Army Service Corps, who came up while I was talking to his officer, saluted, and said in the language of his kind –

"Please, sir, I'm deficient of five mules."

The loss of animals from so small a column is really serious, and everyone is looking blue over his deficiencies. I am deficient of a spade and two nose-bags. But then I am to the good by one lame dog, who, in return for slight services rendered on the road, refuses to allow any but my own lawful servants to approach the encampment. We did eighteen miles to-day, and encamped at Greefdal in the evening. We are now well north of Fourteen Streams, where all day long we have heard the guns booming. In the afternoon the native scouts (who work far outside the ground patrolled by our scouts and flankers) reported a party of 500 Boers approaching from the south and east, but they must have turned northward, for we have heard nothing more of them. This morning we could see a long line of dust moving about twenty miles to the north-east; but it has subsided, and the Boers are probably in laager. It is fortunate that Colonel Mahon is an absolutely careful man, since any little neglect in the matter of patrolling and choosing bivouac positions might mean complete disaster to the column, and the frustration of its end. These little things have often been neglected in this campaign; and whenever there has been a convoy captured, it has been because someone has taken for granted that someone else was holding a drift or pass. So we move warily through a placid country that may become at any moment full of menace; travelling may at any moment be exchanged for fighting, and the roadway for the battlefield; even the green slopes that front us may hide the gravest danger, and the river-bed with its grasses and lapsing waters become a pit of death. But one knows little of the future; it is on the knees of the gods.

CHAPTER XX

From Taungs to Vryburg

DRY HARTZ, *Tuesday, May 8th.*

The march of yesterday afternoon was not without its incidents. We came in sight of the village of Taungs at about four o'clock, our road passing ten miles to the west of it at the opposite side of the Hartz valley. I was riding with the advance guard when a man rode up from the direction of the village.

"I've just come to have a look at the troops," said he; "I'm a British subject."

"Oh, are you?" said the colonel in command of the guard, and ordered him to be detained and examined. He told us a great many lies, and is now a prisoner. We have collected about nine prisoners so far, chiefly insurgents against whom there is grave evidence; and they ride along in an ox-waggon quite contentedly, while the dozen men of the Scots Fusiliers who act as their escort regale them with specimens of northern wit. To judge by the sounds of hilarity which float from the waggon, even towards the end of a long march, their efforts are well appreciated.

A patrol was sent over to Taungs, and we watched the squadron dancing away until a fold of the green plain hid them. Soon afterwards we came into camp.

The paramount question at such a moment is always: "What is the water like?" Last night it was very bad, and there was no officer in charge of the watering when the rear of the column came in. The only water was a small, almost stagnant river, and the men were into it, bathing, as soon as they arrived. Then the horses and mules were watered, and stirred up the mud with their feet; and then we sent for drinking water. Of course one has it boiled, but even so----.

While we were having dinner the patrol returned from Taungs, having cut the wire north and south and destroyed the instrument. They found the village empty except for women.

Encounters with insurgents are often amusing, although amongst them they have so far afforded natives of all our three kingdoms reason for shame. Here is something quite typical.

SCENE: *The veldt road. Enter very slowly from the north, an ox-waggon. Enter from the south, a cloud of dust, out of which emerges the Mounted Advance Guard of the column. They meet, and halt.*

TROOPER *in charge of ox-waggon, saluting and pointing with his thumb within:*

"Come to report, sir. Found this woman trekkin' along, and won't give no account of herself."

Commanding Officer draws aside tent of waggon and discovers fat and hearty old woman.

C.O.: "Now, my good woman, what have you to say for yourself?" (*No answer.*)

TROOPER: "Please, sir, she come from that there rebel farm." (*To fat and hearty old woman*) "Now then, missus, tell the Colonel who you are." (*Long silence, during which something seems to be working in the mind of the fat and hearty old woman.*)

C.O.: "Can anyone speak Dutch? Here, Evans, ask her what she has to say for herself." (*Trooper Evans asks her in fluent Dutch – no answer – question repeated with emphasis.*)

F. and H.O.W.: "Whethen now, and shure it's Mrs. McGuire Oi am, and bad luck to the whole av ye. Glory be to Goodness, but it's a quare place Oi'd be in if the likes of you was all Oi had to me back, wid all me bits av sticks and the ould hin herself took be the Boers – bad cess to 'em" (*and much more to the same effect, during which the waggon is searched and a couple of Martini rifles found in it, and various other damning evidences, with the result that the waggon is confiscated, and the fat and hearty old woman bundled off to her farm, protesting loudly*).

But although such incidents are sometimes amusing they are often painful, and the burning of houses that has gone on this afternoon has been a most unpleasant business. We have been marching through a part of the country where some mischievous person has been collecting and encouraging insurgents. And this afternoon in the course of about ten miles we have burned no less than six farmhouses. Care seems to have been taken that there was proper evidence against the owners who were absent. In one case the wife of an insurgent who was lying sick at a friend's farm, watched from her sick husband's bedside the burning of her home a hundred yards away. I cannot think that punishment need take this wild form; it seems as though a kind of domestic murder were being committed while one watches the roof and furniture of a house blazing; and how many obscure deaths of the soul take place while a woman watches her home, and all the little valueless possessions that are precious to her, falling into ruin before her eyes? I stood till late last night before the red blaze, and saw the flames lick round each piece of the poor furniture – the chairs and tables, the baby's cradle, the chest of drawers containing a world of treasure; and when I saw the poor housewife's face pressed against the window of the neighbouring house my own heart burned with a sense of outrage. The crime of insurrection is a serious one, but I never heard yet of a crime for which the responsibility rested on the criminal alone.

On quite different grounds, this destruction would appear to be worse than useless. The effect on those of the Colonial troops who, in carrying out the orders to destroy, are gratifying their feelings of hatred and revenge, is very bad. Their discipline is far below that of the Imperial troops, and they soon get out of hand. They swarm into the houses, looting and destroying, and filling the air with high-sounding cries of vengeance, and yesterday some of them were complaining bitterly that a suspected house, against the owner of which there was not sufficient evidence, was not delivered into their hands. Further, if these farms are to be confiscated (as the more revengeful loyalists desire) and given over to settlers, why burn the houses? The new occupant will only have to build another homestead, and building is a serious matter where wood and the means of dressing stone are so very scarce as here. The ends achieved are small – simply an exhibition of power, and punishment which (if it be really necessary) could be otherwise inflicted; and the evils, as one sees them on the spot, are many and great. If I described one-half of the little things which I saw in the process of destruction I should be accused of sentimentalising; but the principle of the thing seems clear enough. If one could only hope that with the conflagration would die down those hotter fires that burn in the heart of this country, one might accept the manifest disadvantages. But good feeling will never spring from ashes like these; every charred spot is the grave of that which neither time nor laws can revive.

BRAKFONTEIN, *Wednesday, May 9th.*

We are not far from Vryburg now, and expect to enter it to-day without opposition. From several prisoners taken on the way (there are twenty of them now) we heard that the Boer police in Vryburg knew of our presence at two o'clock on Sunday, and that they all fled. Another farm was burned this morning, and much ammunition destroyed. We have now got over a great and critical part of our journey, which has been admirably made through very difficult country, and we do not expect opposition until we approach Mafeking. Cronje, who was reported on Sunday to be moving westwards with a force to cut us off, has apparently missed us, and he will hardly attempt a rear-guard action without guns. We have two pom-poms, and everyone – even the most peaceful of us – who has once been shot at by these infernal machines is eager to watch them at work from the right end.

VRYBURG, *Thursday, May 10th.*

We occupied Vryburg yesterday at about three o'clock. We made a very easy march, with a long rest at midday, and as the column wound up to the summit of a high ridge we saw Vryburg lying green and white on the farther slope. Half our journey done, and the most dangerous half; it was a pleasant sight. The Boers had all left the little town, and the English residents – chiefly women of the artisan and shopkeeper class – swarmed out to meet us, waving spurious Union Jacks, and exhibiting all the loyalty that can be displayed by means of dyes and pigments. It was like Bloemfontein on a smaller scale.

The people here have been in rather a bad way. There has been a great deal of sickness; the supplies have been very scanty, and meal seems to be the only thing of which they have plenty. So naturally they welcomed the column as the sign of an open road to Kimberley.

I went to see the railway station, which has been much damaged. The only two locomotives here have been outraged; vacuum gauges have been broken, dome-covers torn, and taps smashed; and bullets have been fired at the steel-plated boilers, which, however, they did not penetrate. But it is only outrage, and it seems that with materials left in the workshops here the engines can be repaired in a couple of days. The Boers have been very clumsy over this; a dynamite cartridge might have been strapped under a driving axle in far less time, and its explosion would have been more effectual.

Our chief joy has been in straying about the town, revelling in the sense of things to be bought. No man can withstand shops after having experienced for several days conditions under which money is not of value. There is really nothing to buy that is of much use, but we stand agape at the window of an ironmonger's shop, fingering the money in our pockets, and wondering whether to buy an axe or a mincing machine. On the whole, the axe has it; one must have fires; and bully beef *can* be eaten in the slab form.

CHAPTER XXI

Nearing the Goal

JACKAL'S PAN, *Saturday, May 12th.*

Colonel Mahon's column left Vryburg on Thursday at sunset in a cloud of purple dust, and as long as the light lasted, we could see the rather pathetic-looking little crowd of residents waving handkerchiefs and flags. It was intended only to march for three hours; but our information about water proved to be incorrect, and the column wound along in the moonlight over mile after mile of the most sterile veldt I have yet seen in the country. I was riding with Colonel Mahon for the last few hours, and was to some extent buoyed up by the repeated assurances of the guide that there was water "just round the bend"; but even so it was a weary correspondent who got off his horse at 2 a.m., after eight hours of walking and riding at a foot-pace. Of course, the poor mules suffered most. Even four hours in harness without a rest is considered too much for them; here they had twice that time, over very rough ground, and in consequence half of them had bad breast-galls. It was a mistake to go on for so long, especially as we had to halt after all without water; but the Colonel could not be persuaded to halt until his transport officer warned him that the mules were at the end of their endurance. And all through that weary march no lights were permitted; no smoking even, which gives one something to do; and when we got into the bivouac at two o'clock, no fires or lights. We had to be up at five and start in the misery of darkness and intense cold; without even the comfort of a hot drink; but we reached the water at eight, and had a long morning of rest and sunshine. No one really grumbles at this sort of thing, although it is most unpleasant; and as the men are all picked for health and endurance, no one is any the worse for it.

We marched eighteen miles on Thursday night, and four the next morning; thirteen yesterday evening, and eight this morning; this afternoon we expect to do another twelve, and reduce the distance before us to an easy two days' journey. Of course, all this speed is achieved at a certain cost in mule and horse flesh, but we hope that the end will justify it. The authorities at Kimberley have not done so well for us as they might have done. They did not take the trouble to find out exactly how many horses were in the force, with the result that the daily horse ration has been reduced from the inadequate seven pounds to the absurd four pounds, while the men are on half meat and three-quarter biscuit rations. Another serious defect in the equipment of the column is that there is not even a section of engineers with us. The want is the more felt as water is scarce and bad along the route; often the only water is a small pan or pond into which the mules wade breast high and churn it into mud, which the men have to make a shift to drink. A few sappers and a waggon with the advance guard would ensure a clean supply for everyone, since water that is quite insufficient in a dam can be made to go a long way when it is pumped into watering troughs; and a section of engineers can fix up the whole necessary apparatus in ten minutes.

Far more interesting than the march of a great army corps, where one gets lost in the miles of transport, is the progress of a small column like this, where one is more or less in touch with everyone, and can watch from within the deliberations and methods of the small staff to whom success or failure means so very much. The little group that rides in front of the guns discusses minutely many questions of absorbing interest in the course of a day's march. Whether such and such a ridge ought to be patrolled; how far the scouts are working in this or that direction; whether it is advisable to halt now and go on after a rest, or do a greater distance and have a long rest at the end. And then, when the time for the five minutes' rest in the hour has arrived, "*Halt!*" is passed down the column, and one hears the word running down squadron after squadron until it is lost among the lines of the ammunition column. The connecting files pass it forward to the advance guard, who send it out to their scouts and patrols, until the great serpent that winds over the country is completely at rest. Then follows a sound of horses cropping grass and men talking. Then "*Stand to your horses!*" runs down the column, followed by a shuffling of feet as men scramble from the ground where they have been lying; "*Prepare to mount!*" and there is a general gathering up of reins; "*Mount!*" and a long rustle and jingle as the men swing into their saddles; "*Walk march!*" and the serpent is off again, feeling his way before him.

Three miles in front of us the furthest scouts of the advance guard are working cautiously in the bush, and from the officer in command of the guard a note occasionally comes back to the Brigadier, carried from squadron to squadron and passed along the connecting files until it reaches the head of the main column. One never becomes accustomed to the interest and mystery attaching to these notes, and one almost holds one's breath while they are read; they may contain so much, may carry news of the gravest or most astonishing nature; for if the advance guard found the enemy in strength standing on his head in a donga the information would still be conveyed through the cold propriety of Army Form No. C 398. It is one of the sanest of cold-blooded regulations; let a patrol be never so hard pressed and requiring help never so urgently, the officer commanding it must take time to say so in writing.

I am glad to see that no more farms are being burned, and that we are not burdening ourselves further with the insurgent prisoners. We have already twenty-five, but the Brigadier has been content to read the insurgents who have been taken since a lecture on the folly of their ways, and to warn them that a day of reckoning is coming. I came up to a house yesterday where the Dutch farmer, who was known to be disloyal, had just been arrested and taken away. The troops were making preparations to burn the house, acting on the general order, which had not been cancelled. Within, a child had dropped his toys to stare in astonishment at the strangers, and his mother was weeping alone. I rode back to the Brigadier and said what I could, with the result that I was able to return and assure the woman that her house would not be burned, and in addition to see her husband come back in half an hour. The effect has really been produced already, and prisoners in a flying column are a particular nuisance.

BRODIE'S FARM, *Sunday, May 13th.*

The end is drawing near now, and a fight is almost certain this afternoon or to-morrow. A commando of Boers, 400 strong, was reported yesterday afternoon about eighteen miles on our right flank, and some time during last night they pushed on and occupied a kopje at Koodoesrand, directly in our path, where they laid an ambuscade with three guns. They expected (as well they might) that we should come on and butt into their position. But we have learned our lesson, and this morning we made a detour and have got past them. We have marched nine miles; we shall reach the next water (twelve miles) this evening, and to-morrow we must march straight on to Mafeking (twenty-four miles), for there is no water all the way, and there is the prospect of heavy fighting at the end of it. The horses will simply be used up, but that cannot be helped; if we win it will not matter, and if we lose----. It will be a trying day for everyone, and we shall only have a few hours' sleep to-night, but I think no one grudges the discomfort. I write on the eve of what may be a very brilliant, a very disastrous, or a very simple affair. We are a small force, the march so far has been brilliant, and success will be a brilliant crown for the expedition and its leader. Everyone is more than a little anxious, but it is hard to foretell any result.

I forgot to say that we had a runner from Mafeking, with messages from Colonel Plumer and Colonel Baden-Powell; they asked us what our numbers were, how many our guns, and what the state of our supplies. The answer was most ingenious, as we had no code to which they had a key, and we could not trust a straightforward statement of such important facts to the risks of the road. So Colonel Rhodes invented this answer: –

"Our numbers are the Naval and Military multiplied by ten; our guns, the number of sons in the Ward family; our supplies, the O.C. 9th Lancers."

Excellent as the Boer Intelligence is, I do not suppose that they are aware that the Naval and Military Club is at 94, Piccadilly; that the house of Dudley rejoices in six stalwart sons; or that the officer commanding the 9th Lancers is Colonel Little.

CHAPTER XXII

We Repel an Attack and Join Forces With Plumer

BUCK REEF FARM, *Monday, May 14th.*

A diary is the last place in which to indulge in prophecy; it preserves too clearly the record of fallacy. In the last twenty-four hours have been reversed all the expectations of those in charge of this column, and even the direction of our march has been completely changed. My last entry was made at midday yesterday, and at 2.30 we resumed the march northwards, intending to reach a point ten miles distant at which there was water. The road was very heavy, or rather there was no road at all, the way lying over rough bush veldt, which consists of long, rank grass, with thorn bushes at small intervals and hardwood trees at greater distances – the whole something like an English paddock or park of young trees, except, of course, for the grass. This was heavy going; the mules were hot and tired, and the convoy trailed out and straggled; we spent quite two hours in covering the first four miles.

I have said that the convoy straggled, and there were long intervals between one part of it and the next. During one such interval, the afternoon being very hot, I lay down under a tree and left my horse to graze. A cloud of locusts flying high and beating the air with millions of wings made a pleasant sound as of wind in a forest, and listening to these and to the thousand other minute noises that proceed from the insect life on a few square yards of veldt, I almost fell asleep. There was not a sound from the column; you could not imagine a more peaceful spot; and the obvious contrast between the purpose of this little army and its present circumstances impressed me more vividly than ever. And in less than half an hour from that moment of absolute peace the bullets were hailing round us and the air was resonant with the boom of guns. This is how it happened.

It was half-past three when I left the shade of the tree and joined Colonel Mahon in front of the Horse Artillery, and at twenty minutes to four we heard the sound of rifle-shots – three or four – to the south-east. We had now got into a kind of wood in the bush, and here and there could see beyond the edge of it eastwards towards a hillside that sloped up from us to a ridge four miles away. On this ridge we could see a cloud of dust, and we were looking at it through glasses when a note came in from the right flank reporting a body of the enemy advancing on us from the east. Presently we made out on the edge of the dust a line of horsemen opening out on a kind of glade on the hillside, and the Brigadier ordered the guns to come into position where we were standing. It was really no sort of position at all, being merely a wood with no view from it, and in a hollow at that; but it was all that could be done.

The guns came galloping up, the horses as keen as mustard; in five minutes they had unlimbered and were in position; but Major Jackson, who was in command of the battery, reported that the range was extreme and that he could not be effective. So we lit pipes and waited, while the convoy was ordered to be hurried up as much as possible.

Up galloped an orderly with a note, and everyone tried to read the Brigadier's face. It clouded a little.

"Enemy advancing in strength on our front" was the essence of the note. But "They've got us in the nastiest place of the whole march" was all he said.

In a few minutes more Prince Alexander of Teck came up to report that the convoy was well up, and just as he had finished speaking rifle-fire broke out on our right, and a minute later, sharply, on our front. It was then 4.45, and a bewildering moment for the Brigadier, who had a great, bulky convoy to protect, and had it at the moment in a defenceless position. I think I would not take any reward to bear the responsibility of acting at such a moment. The shots were sounding quicker, but one could see nothing except the surrounding trees. Colonel Mahon looked coolly round.

"We must try with the guns," he said, and ordered another squadron out on the right.

The orderly rode away with the order, and at exactly five o'clock the fire broke out furiously and bullets began to whistle over us. Everyone put his horse into a canter by instinct, and I think the staff went round to the guns. I returned to the convoy to look after my cart.

The convoy was moving on now on as broad a front as the shrubs and trees would permit of; it raised a cloud of dust, which the level rays of the sun lit like a rainbow, and the bullets began to come in a hail. Well, that is rather exaggerated – not a hail. But on a summer day after oppressive heat and dark clouds the big raindrops begin to splash on the ground; and this fire, which many old stagers who have been through several fights describe as the hottest they have known, was something like that. There was no cover; everyone was under fire; so there was nothing to do but to dismount and lead one's horse along beside the convoy. Every now and then with the clear high "phit" of the Mauser bullet would come the hideous twisting whistle of the Martini – really a horrible sound. There was something like a panic amongst the native drivers; they walked along bent almost double, taking what shelter they could; one I saw crawling along on his belly, and the sight made me laugh, although I had at heart too much sympathy with him to be really amused. The mules and horses, alarmed by these strange whistlings in the air, began to neigh and scream, and they added to the general tumult. One gave up wondering whether or no one would be hit, but merely wondered if it would be a graze or a "plug." There were the usual number of miraculous escapes; the driver of the waggon beside which I was walking tumbled off his seat like a sack, stone dead; a mule in the waggon behind me leapt and kicked, and sank on the ground; my horse jumped as a Martini bullet smote the sand at his heel; yet I think there was never a bullet nearer me than a dozen feet. Major Baden-Powell, who is accompanying the expedition for his brother's relief, had his watch, worn in the left breast-pocket, smashed to atoms, but his skin was not even scratched.

They were ten very long and, to put it frankly, very hateful minutes that passed until M Battery opened with a roar. It was a welcome sound, and still more welcome the "pom – pom – pom – *pom*," like the bark of a good dog, that sounded immediately afterwards. And it was like oil on water, or water on fire. Immediately the enemy's fire slackened; in two minutes it had almost ceased; in five it had stopped entirely, and one began to get one's breath. There were men lying all round and about the wood, and the small ambulance staff had more work than they could do; my cart made three trips, carrying wounded men from the column to the dressing-station. Only ten minutes of fighting, and over thirty casualties; six killed, twenty-four wounded, one missing.

But when one had been through those ten minutes, it was not the men lying stark and still in the grass beside the ambulance that made one astonished; it was the sight of people walking about and talking that made one wonder whether or no one had been dreaming. It was decided to halt. Everyone lay down where he stood, and it was a strange, troubled night, with horses stumbling about in the moonlight and blowing with astonishment into one's face.

This morning, as some of us more than half expected, the enemy had cleared, but in consequence of a message received from Colonel Plumer asking us to meet and join him at a certain place we have turned from our original direction. We reached a dry river at eight o'clock this morning, and men had to begin to dig in the sand for water for themselves and their horses. One of my servants found a well fifty feet deep, from which the bucket hoist and ropes were missing. I had sixty feet of rope in my cart, and I went quietly away with two boys carrying all our buckets and bags and kegs, and leading all the horses. We had two hours of very hard work at that well; and when the horses had drunk their fill, and every vessel had been replenished, the fact that there was a well was reported to the Brigadier. In ten minutes a crowd of troopers was round the well, trampling down earth into the water; but if we had only had a few engineers everyone could have been supplied in half an hour.

JAN MASSIBI'S, *Tuesday, May 15th.*

We marched off at half-past three yesterday, keeping west of north; on and on, until half-past eight in the evening. Everyone was dog-tired, and dropped to the ground, only to be roused at one o'clock this morning by the Brigadier, who personally went round and woke people up. He had to shake me twice, and I imagine that other people were wrapped in just as profound an oblivion; nevertheless we were on the march again at 1.30.

Oh, the weariness of that eternal plod through the rough grassy ground, the coldness, the interminable darkness! It was no better on horseback than on foot, for the animals kept falling asleep and stumbling. At every halt one tumbled off one's horse and fell asleep, only to be awakened by the hateful "Stand to your horses." But at last the light began to glimmer in the east, the air took an even colder tone, so that even the grasses seemed to shiver with the breath of dawn, and presently the whole horizon on our right burned with a red fire. Thereafter the shedding of greatcoats and sweaters and woollen helmets, and the glad breathing in of the wine of morning. A little after daylight our advance patrols came in touch with the pickets of Colonel Plumer's camp, down in the valley of the Molopo River at Jan Massibi's. The Brigadier and his staff rode on, and it was a pleasant meeting between the two officers. And pleasanter still when the cloud of dust that heralded our force appeared on the crest of the southern ridge and the long column began to pour down the slope and to cross the drift. Soon it was filling the valley and mingling with the other force already encamped, and now everyone is busy washing or eating near the picturesque little cluster of Kaffir kraals and big shady trees; for the region of karoo and shadeless plain has been left far behind. Our supplies are practically exhausted;

the horses are eating their last ration to-day; but Mafeking is only eighteen miles distant, waiting for our help. There is something inspiring in that knowledge, and in the news of the grand little garrison's latest success; and everyone is anxious to push on and get the inevitable fight over.

To-day we rest under the trees and dream through the music of singing birds, with perhaps a thought for yesterday and the fellow-travellers whose journey ended so suddenly. But for the soldier, more than for anyone, the watchword is "No regrets"; and as for to-morrow, who can tell the issue?

CHAPTER XXIII

The Fighting on the Molopo

At daybreak on Wednesday, May 16th, the two columns under Colonel Mahon's command moved from Jan Massibi's in two parallel lines along the northern bank of the Molopo River. As the sky brightened before us Mafeking was eagerly looked for, but for a long time each successive rise only showed us another beyond which hid the desired view. The country consisted of a succession of ridges lying at right angles to our line of march, and as each one rose before us the staff galloped forward to the summit, only to see another lying beyond. But at last, while some of us were buying eggs at a Kaffir kraal, a more adventurous person climbed upon a rubbish heap and shouted "There's Mafeking!" There was a rush for the coign of vantage, and a great levelling of glasses. There it lay, sure enough, the little town that we had come so far to see – a tiny cluster of white near the eastward horizon, glistening amid the yellowish-brown of the flats. We looked at it for a few moments in silence, and then Colonel Mahon said, "Well, let's be getting on"; and no one said anything more about Mafeking, but everyone thought a great deal.

There was a difficulty about water, and it was finally decided to halt at midday at a point where the Molopo River curved near to the road. We turned off the road down a slope which sank towards the river on the right. The ground rose up on all sides round us, but the guns were placed near the top of the northward rise. The mules were outspanned and led to water, and we breakfasted. Remember that we had been up since half-past five and had had nothing to eat, that it was now nearly an hour after midday, and you will understand how it happened that I was more interested in the cooking of certain meats than in the galloping about of orderlies on the hillside.

Breakfast was just over and my horse was being saddled, when a crack of rifle-fire on our right front warned me that things were about to happen; and at the same time I saw that the mules were being harnessed with frantic haste. By the time that I had ridden up the slope the guns had gone forward into position, but as yet there was no firing except from rifles, which were banging in a desultory fashion now all along our right flank. I searched the slope beyond the river with my glasses, but could not see a man; yet the firing was there sure enough, and increasing. It was at 1.55 that the first firing broke out, and for half an hour the same thing continued, during which the convoy was formed up in what seemed a sheltered part of the hollow. We were in a bad place – a very shallow saucer; and on the edge of the saucer the Boers had taken up their position.

During this half-hour little seemed to be done, but there is always this interval during which a battle develops. We did not as yet know any but one place in which the Boers were; it was pretty certain that they did not know what we were going to do; so the right front, where our advance guard had first come into touch with the enemy, was as yet the only point of contact. Meanwhile Colonel Plumer, with the whole of his mounted men, was sent off to the right flank; Colonel Peakman, with the Kimberley Mounted Corps, was held back to watch the rear; Colonel Edwards was sent with the Imperial Light Horse to the left flank, with instructions to work round in advance if possible, and so turn the enemy's right; and the Royal Horse Artillery and the Canadian guns took up a position on the front. It was difficult to find a place from which to look on, especially as we were far from confident that the Boers were on our right alone. There were folds in the sides of our saucer, and I found a kind of ridge on the northward slope below our guns. I had just dismounted and was watching the right ridge through my glasses when the edge of the horizon at which I was looking was divided by a bright flash. In a few seconds there was a deep report, followed by the whine of a shell in the air; the sand spouted up in a great fountain – Heavens! how close to the convoy; and presently the sound of the burst drowned the crackling of musketry. The convoy huddled away from the smoking patch where the shell had fallen, and began – oh, how slowly! – to wind up the slope towards me. Another shell, still on the same spot, of which the waggons were now quite clear; and now the shells followed each other so rapidly that one gave up trying to distinguish between the initial and the bursting reports, and became absorbed in watching the brown columns spouting from the earth.

They were now playing all round the moving convoy, and each was a miracle; wherever there was a blank space, there the fountain rose; and when the convoy had closed up so completely that one was certain that the next shell must hit something, it fell quite wide. I was still watching this beautiful and dreadful sight when the air above me vibrated to a new song, and on my right a small shell burst with a disagreeable sound. I cleared away to the northern side of the basin, only to feel once more obliged to move as a new gun opened and began to churn up the ground. To be sure, these were long, range-finding shots, and were not intended to pitch where they did, but it is not always safe to rely upon the accuracy of shrapnel fire, and I moved again. But it was of no use; the enemy's pom-pom suddenly began to bark, and played on the one spot which had seemed but a moment before to be safe.

During this development (which had only occupied about ten minutes) our artillery had gradually come into action; first the solitary, abrupt bang of the 12-pound horse gun, then the readier and brisker fusilade of the Canadian quick-firing Vickers-Maxim, then the clamour of our two pom-poms, then the rattle of a Maxim somewhere in the rear. And all the while the area from which the sounds proceeded was spreading like a bush-fire; beginning on the right, it worked across our front, spread from the left front along that flank until it seemed almost to meet the firing on the right rear. When all the guns were going the medley was terrific, although I suppose it was nothing to the sound produced in a really big pitched battle. But it was confusing enough, and, what with the baffling effect of the cross-fire, the whining in the air, and the continuous noise of the explosions, the rattle and crackle of musketry, the galloping hither and thither of orderlies and messengers, and the unpleasantness resulting from the whole thing's happening in so small an area, provided excitement enough to satisfy the most jaded adventurer.

In colder language what had happened was this. The commando that had been holding on for days on our right as we marched had got ahead of us when we diverted towards Plumer, had effected a junction with a force sent out from Mafeking to oppose us, and had just arrived in position near Israel's Farm when we came up against them. Fortunately they had not time to entrench, but they were just going to begin when we turned them, as we found picks and spades lying about in rear of their northward artillery position. From the large outline of their attack there must have been at least 2,000 of them, and from the cleverness with which they were disposed we at first estimated them at twice that number. We held them on our right while we sent a strong force working round on our left, which ultimately got out far enough to turn their right. Of course we were too few to do more than dislodge them; surrounding was out of the question; so when we had fairly turned them we "let go" on the right, and the Boers fled in that direction. The house at Israel's Farm they held until the very end, shelling our rear-guard briskly. The engagement lasted close on five hours, during which our casualties amounted to less than forty.

In even fewer words than these (so concise is his art) the military despatch-writer might have described those eventful hours; and one takes a kind of pleasure in trying to imitate him, so supremely inadequate are such sentences to produce any real impression on people who have never found themselves in the midst of a battle. Not that any art of written words is equal to it. One goes through the whole gamut of sensation; one is charmed, afraid, bewildered; charmed by the scale and magnitude of the operations, afraid for one's own skin, bewildered with a kind of dream at the strangeness of it all. One may sit, as I sat, under a tree listening and watching for hours; and from the grossly and crudely real the thing fades and changes into an unreal image of the senses. The gaudy flies and beetles that hum round one, whose noise is so much louder and nearer than the crash of shells, they fill the foreground of reality; it is not conceivable that the man with the pleasant face and kindly eye who is directing a battery should be attempting the lives of his fellows on so large a scale. Yet it is the scale that makes the difference: a man who would abhor to kill another will with a smile direct the machine that destroys twenty; and he, if anyone, has the right to act upon this reduced estimate of the value of human life, for he counts his own as lightly as that of his enemy.

But I have forsaken my narrative of the fight, and I am confronted by the fact that there are five hours of fighting to be accounted for.

Five hours! Was it for so long that one listened to the voices of guns and rifles? I can hardly believe it, and no bare catalogue of man[oe]uvres seems to fill the gap. Our artillery positions were changed several times, and when the convoy was crowded up into a fold of the ground the shells no longer reached it, but continued to pound at Colonel Peakman and his rear-guard. At about five o'clock, the Boers having cleared from our left front, the convoy was pushed on in that direction, and we penetrated as far as the position which had been held by the Boer 15-pounder on our front. Just as we reached that point a note was brought in from Colonel Plumer on the right reporting that he was checked by the Boers at Israel's Farm, and accordingly the Horse Artillery battery was formed up in front of the convoy, and with the two pom-poms (which followed it about like small dogs barking after a big one) shelled the farm, which the enemy evacuated. The sun began to sink, the firing in our rear dropped and died out gradually, and with a few shots from a Martini, fired by someone on the left who amused himself by sniping the staff, the fight came to an end.

The fight was over, but as the convoy began to work its way cautiously through the bush in the dusk we began to talk about it, and to fit it together from the pieces of our individual experience. What had they been trying to do? What had So-and-so been doing on the left? Had we many casualties? Should we go on into Mafeking? Ah, that was the question. But after about an hour's trekking through the bush it was decided to halt, as someone reported that the enemy was entrenched ahead of us. As for the fight, we did not then fully know what had happened, but we found out afterwards. The Boers had once more given us a lesson in tactics, and we had given them one in dealing with a nasty situation. With a comparatively small force (although stronger than ours) they had bluffed us by extending their attack round a large perimeter, leading us to suppose their strength to be far greater than it really was. They had caught us in the one bad bit of country between Jan Massibi's and Mafeking, and but for the really excellent fighting on our side might have held us where we were until the want of supplies forced us to retire or surrender. As we had so few casualties it is probable that they had not many; but it is possible to have very warm fighting with few casualties. Our cover was excellent; so was theirs; and Colonel Peakman, who, with the rear-guard, bore the heaviest burden of the fight, lost hardly a man, although he lost heavily in horses. Everyone is agreed that the honours of the day fell chiefly to this gallant business man, who in his spare time had made himself so good a soldier.

All these matters were talked over until we halted about seven o'clock and reluctantly heard that we were not to proceed that night. No lights, of course; but everyone was ready to lie down. While my bed was being prepared I went over to the ambulance, whither the wounded were being brought in on stretchers. There were only two small waggons, and the wretched sufferers were literally heaped inside them, lying in the dark amid their own blood. The little staff under Surgeon-Captain Davies worked gallantly, getting the men out, dressing their wounds, making them as comfortable as possible on blankets over the grass; but it was a miserable and sordid scene, relieved only by the cheery willingness of the helpers and the fortitude of the patients. Even here, of course, there were no lights, but in the recesses of a waggon an orderly was trying to prepare hot water with a tiny Etna. Dressing about twenty serious surgical cases out of doors in pitch darkness, with a limited supply of not over clean water, short-handed, hurried, without proper appliances – it was a sight that would have startled the artist in antiseptic surgery. But there they lay; and it was with something like a sense of shame that I turned into my own comfortable bed.

CHAPTER XXIV

Mafeking at Last

They were twenty-four very exciting hours that began when we moved from Jan Massibi's at daybreak on Wednesday and ended when we lay down to snatch a little rest at daybreak on Thursday. Many miles were travelled, a great enterprise was brought to a successful issue, a tough battle was fought, men received wounds and died, Mafeking was relieved: enough incident and adventure to fill months of ordinary life. The bare events are recorded here, but the emotional history of those twenty-four hours will probably never be written. But as you read the narrative, put yourself in the place of those to whom it was not a story but a piece of life, and then perhaps you will realise something of what it meant to them.

Not much of the story remains to be told.

At midnight between Wednesday and Thursday I was awakened by a general stir in the surrounding camp, to find that the moon was shining brightly, lighting up busy drivers, and the troops getting their horses ready. We were to advance. Major Karri-Davies had ridden on into Mafeking, and, with the luck which rewards daring, had found the road clear, and sent back a messenger with that information to Colonel Mahon. I think men were never so willingly awakened from sleep; not even the wounded grumbled, who had also to be roused from their beds on the grass and repacked into the stuffy ambulance. At about 12.30 we were ready to start, but during the first mile there were long halts and delays while the guides argued and boggled about the roads. At last the strain became too great, and Major Gifford, Captain Smith, and I resolved to ride on and trust to finding the right road. We knew the direction by the stars, and started across the veldt a little south of east.

It was bitterly cold, and we were all both sleepy and hungry, but there was an excitement in the air that kept us easily going. After about half an hour we heard voices ahead, and descried the shapes of horses and men. Our hearts sank for a moment, only to rise again when we recognised Colonel Peakman, who, having been in command of the rear-guard on the previous day up till nine o'clock at night, was now taking his turn at advance guard at one o'clock the next morning. As a Kimberley man, it had long been his ambition to lead the relieving force into Mafeking, and I think no one grudged him the honour. Amongst all, indeed, there was a certain amount of competition, and the four correspondents who survived to the end of the expedition became strangely silent about their intentions for the evening. I pinned my faith to Peakman, as I knew he was as anxious as anyone to be in first.

Well, we joined the Advance Guard, which presently went on along the road pointed out by the guide, and for an hour we jogged on at a fast walk, until we had clearly "run the distance," as they say at sea. Still no sign of the trenches or forts which should mark the outward boundary of the defended area. We pulled up, and the guide was questioned.

"Two miles more," he said.

We rode on for another quarter of an hour, and still found nothing before us but the rolling veldt; not a light, not a sound except the beating of the horses' feet. Again we halted, and this time Colonel Peakman himself questioned the guide, and the man had to admit that he had mistaken his way, and that we were on the lower road, longer by a good three miles than that originally intended. We had no connecting files with the main column, and, as it had a guide of its own, it was certain that it would take the shorter road, and probably be in before its own Advance Guard. A bitter moment, in which things were said to the guide; but some of us hoped that the slow convoy, with its tired and galled mules, would even yet take a longer time on its short road than we on our long one. So we went on again, this time at a trot; the excitement seemed to extend to the horses, so that even they could not be restrained. In ten minutes we saw men sitting by the roadside, and found a hundred very weary Fusiliers, who had been sent to take Israel's Farm at the end of the fight, and told to go on afterwards.

"Had anyone passed along the road before us?" "No"; and with a gasp of relief we hurried on. In a few moment's the group in advance pulled up, shouting "'Ware barbed wire!"

We all stopped, and there were frantic calls for wire-cutters. With four reports like the snapping of big fiddle-strings the last barrier before Mafeking was removed, and we passed on again, this time at a hand-canter. In a few minutes we heard the sound of a galloping horse on the road, and a mounted man challenged us.

"Halt! Who goes there?"

"Friend."

"Who are you?" (The excitement was too high for the preservation of the proper formula.)

"Colonel Peakman, in command of the Advance Guard of the Relief Column."

"By Jove, ain't I glad to see you, sir!"

It was an officer sent out by Colonel Baden-Powell to meet us and bring us in. We left the squadron, and the five of us went on, this time at a gallop, over trenches, past breastworks and redoubts and little forts, until we pulled up at the door of the headquarters' mess.

Ah, the narrative is helpless here. No art could describe the handshaking and the welcome and the smiles on the faces of these tired-looking men; how they looked with rapt faces at us commonplace people from the outer world as though we were angels, how we all tried to speak at once, and only succeeded in gazing at each other and in saying, "By Jove!" "Well, I'm hanged!" and the like senseless expressions that sometimes mean much to Englishmen. One man tried to speak; then he swore; then he buried his face in his arms and sobbed. We all gulped at nothing, until someone brought in cocoa and we gulped that instead; then Baden-Powell came in, and one could only gaze at him, and search in vain on his jolly face for the traces of seven months' anxiety and strain.

After an hour we went out and found the column safely encamped just outside the town. Everyone was dog-tired, and although it was half-past five in the morning and the moon was sinking we lay down and were immediately asleep – in Mafeking.

We did not know it, but we were in a besieged town. Officially the relief did not take place until ten o'clock that morning, when the Boers hurried away with their last gun. I was awakened at eight by the sound of heavy firing, and as soon as my horse was ready rode away to the north-east corner of the town (we had entered from the north-west), to where the greater part of our column was in action. Through glasses one could see something being drawn up the purple slope of a hill six miles away – the last gun of the besiegers. Earlier in the morning our troops had advanced on all the Boer positions which were still occupied (only the eastern ones were then held), and had shelled the enemy in the midst of his preparations for flight. It was only a rear-guard action; indeed the engagement was practically limited to the artillery; and all I was in time to see was the flight. It was a good sight, the mounted men galloping in open order up the hillside which the morning sun was throwing into a thousand patches of light and shade. They were soon out of range, and we stood watching the disappearing specks of black crawl like flies up the furthest ridges, here in groups of a dozen, there in twos and threes, until the last one had vanished from our view; and thus the siege of Mafeking came to an end.

There was joy in the camps of the relieving column when it was known that they had also taken part in the siege; "Another bar," said the medal-hunters.

Colonel Mahon's column consisted of 900 mounted men of the Imperial Light Horse, under Lieutenant-Colonel Edwardes, and the amalgamation of local troops known as the Kimberley Mounted Corps, under Colonel King; 100 picked volunteers from the Fusilier Brigade; four guns of M Battery Royal Horse Artillery, under Major Jackson, and a pom-pom section (two guns), under Captain Robinson, the whole artillery force consisting of 100 men; three Maxims, 56 waggons, and several private Cape carts, 660 mules; in all, 1,200 horses and 1,100 men.

The staff was: Colonel Mahon, 8th Hussars, brigadier; Captain Bell-Smythe, 1st Dragoon Guards, chief staff officer; Colonel Frank Rhodes, late Royal Dragoons, chief of Intelligence Department; Prince Alexander of Teck, 7th Hussars, A.D.C.; Major Jackson, commanding Royal Artillery; Major Sir John Willoughby, late of the Blues; Major the Hon. Maurice Gifford, attached to the Imperial Yeomanry, general staff; and Lieutenant F.W. Smith, Kimberley Mounted Corps, galloper. There was not an officer on the staff whose industry and good sense did not contribute to the success of the expedition; and we correspondents owe a peculiar gratitude to Colonel Rhodes, who acted as Press Censor. No doubt his own experience as a correspondent helped him to fulfil what is always a responsible and seldom an easy office. He was always considerate, always interested, always kind and always fair.

Here ends an imperfect narrative of the relief. What the deliverers saw on Thursday morning was a little white town lying in the midst of a wide shallow basin of green moorland; and it reminded one of a town that had been long deserted and in ruins. I am not exaggerating when I say that by far the greater number of houses in the town had been struck by shells, and that very nearly all had been struck either by shells or bullets.

After the engagement on Thursday morning the relieving column formed up and entered the town, headed by Colonel Baden-Powell, Colonel Mahon, and his staff. As one passed house after house, one with a gaping hole in its side, another with the chimneys overthrown, another with a whole wall stove in, none with windows completely glazed, all bearing some mark of assault – as this panorama of destruction unfolded itself one marvelled that anyone should have lived throughout the siege. And when the procession formed up in the dilapidated Market Square, and the whole of the Town Guard mustered – Kaffirs, Parsees, Jews, Arabians, Englishmen, Dutchmen, nearly every sort and nationality of men – and when the Mayor read an address expressing in the conventional terms of such compliments the emotions of this motley crowd, one asked oneself what it was that had held these very ordinary-looking people to so heroic an intention. Remember that the defence of Mafeking had been one big bluff, that there was nothing to prevent the Boers, with determination and careful arrangement, from taking the place at almost any time, and you will realise how startlingly that question asserted itself. I like to think that there were many men in Mafeking whose courage alone would have disdained surrender; but there was one man in whose face one found the answer to the riddle. Brains alone would not have done it; heart alone would have fainted and failed under those long months of danger; but the officer commanding this garrison had both brains and heart, and so he taught his men to endure.

I do not pay the garrison of Mafeking so poor a compliment as to suppose that the mere hunger for luxuries, serious misfortune though it be, was the signal trial of its endurance. Ladysmith suffered worse in this respect and did not complain. In Mafeking there was always a plentiful supply of green vegetables, of tobacco, and of wine, and it was only with a smile that the heir to one of the wealthiest estates in England told me that they had latterly invented a brawn made with glue from the hides and feet and ears of mules and donkeys.

But nearly 30,000 shells fell into a town covering about the same area as Cowes; in many streets not a man dared show himself save under the cloud of a dark night, for they were swept by rifle bullets; hardly one of the many forts on the circumference of defence held weapons half so formidable as the stout hearts that served them. Thirty thousand shells! I have been in the neighbourhood of perhaps a hundred bursting shells, and every burst will be a memory for a lifetime; but thirty thousand! The heart stops at the thought. Yet here was the little ruined town; here were the men with weak bodies and cheery faces to prove that courage can raise the mind beyond fear and suffering; that, given an ideal and a chance in the leadership, men may be counted on for something far greater even than bravery.

CHAPTER XXV

A Memorial of the Siege

There is nothing pretty about the place where the dead defenders of Mafeking are laid. It lies in a little square of brown stone wall, planted amid the dreary waste outside the town. There are no green lawns, no twisted yews, no weeping willows; the few fir trees hold themselves stiffly up, as though in pride at this triumph of the vegetable over the animal; and the great bushes of faded geranium only throw into relief the regular lines of limestone mounds, each with its prim wooden cross of advertisement. Always an ugly and a dreary place, it was, when I saw it a few days after the relief, more dreary than ever; for the sun, whose presence makes the difference of a season in this bare land, was hidden behind dark stacks of cloud flying westward before a cold gale.

From a sandbag protection at one corner of the cemetery there is a view on all sides to the horizon. The town, the empty railway station, the hospital, the network of shelter trenches, connecting earth-works, redans, redoubts, forts, and emplacements; the straight line of railway-ruled across the plain to the horizon – these make the view. Hardly anything is moving except the white flag on the hospital and the colours on the forts. Sometimes a figure crosses the open stretch between the hospital and the town, but outside the cemetery itself hardly a man is to be seen. The wind hums in the empty hearth of a locomotive, through the stiff trees of the cemetery, past the signal, standing like a sentinel gone to sleep with his head sunk on his breast, waiting in an attitude of invitation for the train that is seven months overdue.

One's eye returns along the shining rails until it rests again within the yard, in a far corner of which a couple of orderlies detailed for burial fatigue are hacking with picks at the hard, white earth. The graves are in prim, uniform rows – the soldiers' graves, I mean, for even here the military element swamps the civilian, and one hardly takes note of the private graves, they are so few. But the soldiers' graves are arranged with military precision, row behind row, each row containing twenty graves or more. And at least seven or eight rows of graves are marked by the regulation cross, while there are many rows on which as yet no crosses have been erected. The painted words on the crosses become monotonous as one reads from the head of the first row down to where the mounds give place to gaping caverns – five or six – prepared for the dying, whom even now the doctor is plying with physic in the hospital.

Trooper A, Private B, Colour-Sergeant C; the names vary, indeed, but there are only three versions of the manner of death – "Died of wounds," "Died of enteric fever," "Killed in action" – the three epitaphs for soldiers in South Africa.

It was strange, amid the dreariness and stagnation of this place, to think of the jubilations at home. What cheering, what toasting, what hilarity! But here the sparkle in the wine had died, leaving the cup that had brimmed flat and dull and only half full after all. Food was scanty and of the plainest quality, there was no news from the outside world, disease was still busy; and here, set forth in the hard limestone, was the bill for all the glory and excitement. The bill, but not the payment; that was being made at home by the people who cared for what lies beneath the limestone.

The evils of a war are so direct and obvious that they are apt to be discounted or accepted as Fate, and classed among the thousand unavoidable ills beneath which we must patiently sit. But are they? In a war, the necessity and even justice of which are doubted honestly by many, where all share the responsibility and few the personal cost, it is hard to see the hand of an impartial Fate.

A strange place, you may say, in which to attempt the adjustment of mingled impressions. Yet in the midst of our crude existence at Mafeking, where life was shorn of all the impalpable things that make it real and reduced to a simple material level of food and sleep and noise, it was a kind of relief to spend an hour in the place where men had gone down into rest and silence. In normal circumstances one may avoid such places, but after the din of arms and the shout of victory there was a sense of companionship to be found in the place that stood for the ending of disputes. Peaceful, yes; but how was the peace gained? It is sweet and seemly to die for one's country; but blood and fire, grief and anguish had filled the vestibule of this sleeping-chamber; and peaceful though it be, the graveyard of Mafeking is a place to induce in Englishmen some searchings of heart.

"Oh, surely not," says the music-hall patriot; "the brave fellows who lie there have died a glorious death, and the glory is ours as their fellow-countrymen"; and he drops a tear and a shilling into the particular tambourine which happens at the moment to be raising the loudest clamour, and honestly believes himself to have achieved some nobility at second-hand.

Our glory? Hardly that. Those who, justly or unjustly, place the martyr in his last predicament do not wear his crown; and the glory of Trooper A's death does not rest with you or me, but with those in whose hearts his memory is quick and real. To count these scores of deaths, as it were, to our credit in the war, to esteem them merely as things for which more vengeance must be taken, would be the last and greatest mistake. Surely they lie in the scale of responsibility, they are things for which an account must be rendered, by which an obligation is incurred to use well the fruits of victory.

There is no need that the wind should moan over this desolate patch, or that the tattered geranium should scatter its withered leaves on the unlovely ground. Were it as sweet as a garden in Delos, were the ground carpeted with violet and primrose and shadows of laburnum, the burying-ground of Mafeking would still be a sad spot on the chart of British South Africa.

CHAPTER XXVI

Good-Bye to Mafeking

A sudden order from General Hunter; a morning of preparation; a commotion of dismantling, packing, harnessing, saddling; handshaking and well-wishing; cheers ringing, hoofs clattering, dust rising beneath wheels and many feet, a backward glance along the road, and – Good-bye to Mafeking. An episode in the lives of men, and one which, in spite of the excitement that went before it, will probably leave a small though deep impression. Life there was dull beyond words, perhaps because there must be a reaction after seven months of excitement, and because the nature of man is elastic, springing quickly back to the commonplace when an unusual element in its circumstances has been withdrawn. I tried hard to fancy that the people of the garrison bore in their faces or manners some sign of the strain which they had undergone. But the months seemed to have left no traces except on the buildings and on the cemetery; or perhaps their mark upon the besieged men was set beneath the surface scanned by a casual observer. At any rate, the people of Mafeking could not successfully be exhibited in a show of wonders, and they took less interest in their food than did we, their deliverers, who lived with them for a while in what might be called "poor circumstances." Strange to say, the only way in which to secure an ample meal in Mafeking was to give a dinner-party, when all sorts of things were produced from secret reserves and – charged for.

Brigadier-General Mahon's column left Mafeking on Monday, May 28th, taking the road that runs southward beside the railway, and I think that everyone breathed a sigh of satisfaction when we were once more fairly on the road. "The Happy Family" someone called Mahon's force, and there was certainly never a more united company. He is the kind of leader – considerate, strict, careless of unessential formalities, careful of all essential details, jolly of face, kind of eye, a good companion on the road, a rock of strength and confidence in the field – who is obeyed in the spirit as well as the letter, and for whom men would gladly march their feet to blisters. It need hardly be said that he is an Irishman – "Ould Pat Mahon God bless 'um!" as a friend of mine said that morning; and the remark was strangely apt, in spite of the Brigadier's youth and the fact that his name is Bryan.

For four days we marched southward in easy stages across a stretch of country that was almost blighted by the scarcity of water; we never had water through which the bottom of a white cup could be seen; nearly always we had to share with the mules and horses the vast puddle known in that country as a pan, and at every puddle or waterhole, as the mules churned it up into inky mud, the wish was the same – "If only we had some engineers!"

At Maritsani siding we found the first really serious break in the railway. For about three miles the line was completely wrecked, and two culverts, one (over the river) spanned by unusually long girders, had been blasted in the middle and were lying broken in the gap. Even here it was easy to distinguish between the work of the trained German or French engineer and that of the ordinary rank-and-file Boer. The Boer did not understand dynamite, but he had a very fair idea of destruction from the spectacular point of view, and his work made by far the finer show. One might almost think that children had been at work, so laborious and futile were his efforts. The permanent way for perhaps two miles was bodily uprooted, each length of rails with the sleepers attached, and laid along the embankment. Not a thing was destroyed; the fishplates, four to each joint, were lying at a convenient distance, and even the bolts and nuts for securing them were disposed in little heaps. All that the repairing party had to do there was to replace the lengths of line, couple them, and shovel in the ballast. But the mile on which the trained engineer had been at work probably took four times as long to repair. Here a dynamite cap had been attached to the middle of each rail, with the result that there was a piece about six inches long blown out of every length, and that meant that all the old way had to be taken up and an entirely new one laid down. One thing I did envy this simple-minded enemy of ours, and that was the pleasure he must have experienced in doing one bit of damage. Towards one culvert the line sloped down in a long gradient, and on this a couple of trucks and a van had evidently been placed and allowed to run down to the culvert, where, the bridge being gone, they plunged into the gap. Think of the glorious smash! The trucks must have got up considerable speed. And picture the crowd waiting expectantly for the final catastrophe. I must say that I should have liked to see it.

The destructive spirit had evidently been satisfied by this gorgeous sacrifice, for nine miles of the line and telegraph wires running southward from Maritsani were untouched, and at Kraaipan, where we met the repairing party from the south, the damage was nearly repaired.

On the Thursday night we marched from Kraaipan to a point four miles north of Maribogo station, and during the march we heard a whistle in the far distance. A message was sent to the advance guard, and the train was "held up" while we gleaned some news from the officer in charge. To us who had been living in the wild for more than a month the great hot, hissing, bubbling engine was a strange sight, and we stood gazing at it open-mouthed like yokels, and stretching out our hands towards its warm body. When we had learned the news it moved off into the darkness with a shriek, and we resumed our march with a strange sense of cold and silence. Early next morning (June 1st) the column marched into Maribogo, where it was to receive ten days' provisions and a complete supply of remounts – new wings for the flying column. Hunter and the components of his force were to rendezvous at Lichtenburg on June 7th.

Setting out from Maribogo on Sunday morning, June 3rd, we entered the Transvaal at about midday, and reached Geysdorp in the afternoon. Hart's brigade had left Maribogo a few hours before us, and we passed ahead of it at Geysdorp. After having been long with only mounted troops we thought the infantry brigade a slow and primitive thing; but we envied it the drums and fifes, to the music of which the Irishmen were stepping along bravely when we passed. Although their destination, like ours, was Lichtenburg, we marched at different times of the day, for even in this large country there was not room on the road for both brigades. While they were yet asleep in their bivouacs we were at breakfast, and their reveille generally found us setting out on the march.

The awaking of a column on these dark, cold mornings is ghostly and mysterious. The first trumpet-call trembling through the chill starlight brings one back from dreams to the world. The cavalry trumpeter plays a longer and more ornate flourish than that sounded by the infantry bugler, but reveille is all too short on a winter morning. From under one's shelter one sees the camp return to life – first a match glowing here, then the smoke and crackle of a fire there, until acres of ground are scattered with flame. Then the sound of voices begins to insinuate itself – one never knows exactly when it begins – until the air is lively with the cries of the cheerful Kaffir. Darkness still on the ground and cold starlight in the upper air; but eastwards a very sharp eye might notice a kind of lightening of the gloom. And cold, bitterly cold, one gratefully withdraws beneath blankets the hand that was experimentally stretched out. In one's own little camp the stir is also beginning; fires being kindled, shadowy figures moving through the gloom, the sound of horses munching corn. Presently the air vibrates to another trumpet-call – "Stables"; and the few horses (chiefly among the artillery) that know the calls begin to neigh and paw the ground. Now the sky above the eastward horizon has faded to the palest blue, revealing the heads of horses and men where one thought there were only trees, and along the lower edge of the blue comes another line, like a fine silver wire. It grows broader and fades into the blue, but in its place comes a sheet of dull crimson. Millions of miles away God sets it on fire, and it kindles, glows, flushes to scarlet, melts into gold, until from the gold flows amber, and from amber the pure white wine of daylight. All the old colours rush westward across the sky; the veldt glows with tints that have no name nor description in our dull tongue; yet these are the mere drip and overflow of the dayspring.

Small wonder if amid such an entertainment one forgets the bustle in the now visible camp, and smaller still if one forgets that one ever wanted to sleep. Another trumpet sounds – "Boot and saddle" – and the bustle becomes acute as the mules are harnessed and horses saddled. And from some near squadron which is to form the advance guard are heard the few sharp orders that are necessary to transform it from a crowd of men and horses to a military unit. "Fall in. Number!" And the numbers run down a switchback of sound as each man shouts his own. "Stand to your horses. Prepare to mount. Mount. Advance by sections from the right. Walk – march!" And with the last word the day's work begins.

On Tuesday morning I had ridden on far in advance of the column in search of buck. There was very little cover, and at the first shot they were off like the wind, so I gave it up. Just beyond the ridge where I had been shooting I came upon the pan of water that was to be our outspan, and beside the pan was a farmhouse, outside of which stood a little group of people. An old woman, a young man, a girl, two middle-aged matrons, a man horribly deformed – people of different ages and manners, yet having in common one startling thing: they were all shaking with terror. It was startling because they were the only living creatures except birds and springbuck that I had seen for miles of that lonely march. The heath stretching to the sky north and south and east and west; the muddy pan; the poor house and outbuildings; the solitary horseman; the terrified group – these filled the picture; and it was not without misgivings that I approached the house.

"Oh, sir" (it was one of the matrons speaking English with the pleasant deliberation of a Dutchwoman), "was it you whom we heard shooting on the hill?"

When I said that it was they all gasped with relief, and the women broke out into a clamour of talk and questioning. Was the army coming? Were there many troops? Where were the Kaffirs? Was I sure that there were no Kaffirs about? When I had reassured them on the point the deformed man spoke.

"The Kaffirs are jumping about. Ja! They have looted my farm. All my stock also. We are afraid. I am waiting to go to my farm, which is one hour over the hill, but when I heard your gun I was afraid the Kaffirs were near. They know we are only women or sick men here, and they have guns, and they are jumping about. Your Colonel at Mafeking gave them guns, and now they run about stealing and murdering. All last night I dared not move from here, although we have no food. I was afraid, and so were these ladies, knowing they were jumping about. Now I go to my farm."

He called a black boy, who presently brought round a miserable cart drawn by two skeleton ponies. One of the women got in. There was no need to ask the fierce little cripple why he had not been on commando, and I was wondering how he was going to get into the cart, when he gave a great leap, and, climbing nimbly into his seat, drove away.

When he had gone the woman of the house began to pour out a woeful tale. Her husband – was he dead or alive? No news for three months; no letters or telegrams. Even the casualty lists had ceased to reach them. Her babe was dying for want of milk food. Could I give her a tin? General Hunter's men had broken up her kraal to use the wood for burning, and all her goats had wandered off and she had no one to send to look for them. These few logs of wood were all she had to bake bread with; would I ask the General to see that the soldiers did not take them? And then the Kaffirs! It was a piteous tale launched on a flood of tears. Possibly it was exaggerated; people have different ways of asking for help; but the terror in the woman's eye when she spoke of the Kaffirs was genuine. And I remembered the cripple's phrase – "The Kaffirs are jumping about."

Captain Bell-Smythe, the brigade major, came up presently, and I found him willing, as he and General Mahon had always been, to listen with patience to the long recital of woe. A sentry was put over the house and gardens to protect them from the desecrating foot of Tommy, and I know that a tin of milk was furnished out of the scanty stores of the headquarters' mess.

As for the Kaffirs, that trouble turned out to be a very real one. On the next day's march four were captured by a patrol of General Barton and shot, and it almost seems as though their blood were upon the heads of those who failed to disarm them after the siege of Mafeking was raised. I heard that the reason given was that it would offend the Barralongs, who had fought so bravely in defence of their staadt; but surely it had been better to offend them than allow them to run their heads into a noose. The Kaffir trouble was like a shadow on our march; they imagined that they had old scores to pay off; they paid them with remarkable fidelity to their own austere sense of justice; and it was felt that in suffering death they were bearing the punishment for more than their own misdeeds.

Incidents such as these marked the days of our march to Lichtenburg. But our family was breaking up; Colonel Rhodes and Sir John Willoughby, who had worked so hard on the relieving march, left us at Maribogo; one by one my fellow-correspondents were departing; one officer after another who had been with us on some special service was being withdrawn.

And suddenly my own summons came. Over thousands of miles of sea-bed it found me at a spot where the telegraph instruments never spoke before, and may never speak again until the end of Time. We were encamped fifteen miles from Lichtenburg, in a place made green by a clear and brimming river. I had wished to send a telegram, and the obliging orderly had undertaken to tap the temporary wire and "call up" Lichtenburg. So the instruments were connected in the green field, and soon the voice of the man at Lichtenburg was heard. The first thing he did was to ask if anyone of my name was with the column, and when he found I was there he said there was a cable for me. He read it to me over the wire, with the result that I did not send my telegram. And presently the voice ceased, the wire was disconnected, and (although I had been hoping that the message would come) I went about like one under sentence of death.

We came on into Lichtenburg the next day, once more passing the Irish Brigade with its childish pipes. General Hunter's division was now complete, and I had not seen so great an encampment of tents since leaving Lord Methuen at Boshof. They surrounded the pretty town – long lanes arched by great willows trembling over streams such as run clearly through the streets of all South African villages. On the next day Mahon's column, proceeding in advance of the Division, was to set out towards Rustenburg, while I rode forty miles westward into Mafeking.

The day at Lichtenburg was very busy, occupied by those miserable duties that affront the softer feelings. To dismantle and sell the moving home that, as though by a miracle, has been nightly disposed through hundreds of miles of road travel, and to part from horses that have served you well and shared your dangers, if not your alarms, is to suffer a new and painful damage to the affections. It was here, also, that I had to say good-bye to Major Pollock, with whom I had been living for the last five months. Some correspondents live always alone, and some like to join with several of their fellows in a large mess; but I think that our arrangement (when one is so fortunate in one's companion as I was) is by far the best. Of course the newspaper correspondent has to remember that he is the rival and not the ally of all his fellows; but in the South African war there were many occasions when two correspondents might work together to the advantage of both newspapers, and there were few occasions when a correspondent could obtain any advantage or information which was not shared by all the rest. At such times, of course, when they did arise, we used to become very silent as to our immediate intentions, and the subject which was uppermost in both our minds was shunned. But so long as my companion was with me I never lacked a home on the veldt.

The happiest endings and the lightest farewells are indeed serious; they punctuate life, and set a period upon chapters that may not be revised. Out of the dust of preparation rose once more the pillar of cloud that had hovered over the column for hundreds of dusty miles; and soon to an accompaniment of stamping feet and jingling harness it moved on, leaving me behind as it had left so many others – not all to go home, but some to sleep beneath the roadside bushes. General Mahon waited, chatting, until the last waggon had passed, and then he also, who had been the pleasantest of companions as well as the most respected of commanding officers, rode away with that stiffening of the back with which your true soldier ever turns from private to public affairs. I looked after the vanishing column, and felt as though every prop of existence had been knocked from under me. I had been one amongst a thousand, a mere molecule in a large mass, moved hither and thither without reference to my desires or efforts; and I resented the restoration of independence. Strange contradiction! We crave and struggle for individuality; here was mine restored to me, and I looked at it askance. The tail of the column disappeared round a bend in the road. Was this indeed the end of the chapter?

Not quite the end. As I set out on the westward road I met a half-battalion of the Scots Fusiliers returning to camp from exercise, marching at ease. Each company was headed by a piper who swung and swaggered, blowing deep into the lungs of his instrument. As one company passed, the measured bleat and squeal of the pipes faded and merged into a sound heralding the approach of another. The gorgeous uniforms were absent; but even the shabby khaki, stained with the soil of long marches and hard fights, could not obliterate that perfect harmony of movement which marks the first-class regiment.

I stood to watch them go by. The last company approached; the piper, his head thrown back, so deeply drunk of sound that his soul seemed to float on the steady hum of the chanter, set the rhythm to ranks of men stepping out to the inspiring discord. I turned my horse's head; before me the road stretched long and lonely; behind was the bustle and stir of the camp. A file of officers marching behind the column hailed me with envious congratulation when they heard where I was going. But they did not know that, just for one moment, I would have given the world to turn and follow the piper.

THE END.

Lightning Source UK Ltd.
Milton Keynes UK
18 December 2010

164586UK00001B/75/P